BURN THE BOATS

A Seven-Championship Season for Boston University Hockey

Scott Weighart

The Inside Story of the 2008-09 Terriers

Featuring Photography by Gil Talbot, Dominick Reuter, and Josh Gibney

First Edition
Copyright © 2009 by Scott Weighart

Cover design by Victoria Arico

ISBN: 978-0-9621264-7-5

Printed in the United States of America

For Hannah and Timmy, who attended their first Boston University hockey games before they could crawl.

CONTENTS

ACKNOWLEDGEMENTS

First, thanks to the Boston University hockey program for pulling out a victory in the national championship game. While I had considered writing this book since January of 2008, I had concluded that the idea was a non-starter if the Terriers did not go all the way.

This book also would not exist without the support and cooperation of Terrier head coach Jack Parker and BU athletic director Mike Lynch. BU's senior assistant director of athletic communications Brian Kelley also played a key role in the book's creation as the point person in coordinating the many interviews and myriad logistical necessities—including my press credentials for the Frozen Four. I am extremely grateful for his ongoing support, including a thorough proofreading of this book. Thanks also to Dan Satter from BU's athletic department for his considerable assistance with proofreading as well. Many Terrier players and coaches—too numerous to mention here—agreed to the lengthy and candid interviews that added much color to this book. In addition, Bernie Corbett, Kathi Brown, and Anne Lawrence contributed anecdotes for the story, while captain-elect Kevin Shattenkirk read an early draft to ensure that the content was on target.

As you can see on the front and back covers as well as in the 16-page spread of color photos, the three photographers featured here—Dominick Reuter, Gil Talbot, and Josh Gibney—have added a great deal to this project with their fine work. If you would like to see more of their work and/or inquire about purchasing individual prints, check out their websites:

- http://www.dominickreuter.com/
- http://www.giltalbot.com/
- http://www.joshgibney.com/

I was thrilled that Vicky Arico was willing to design the front and back covers of this book. I think she surprised herself this time by coming up with this "fire and ice" theme so quickly and effectively.

Nancy Marrapese-Burrell of *The Boston Globe* not only agreed to write a thoughtful and flattering blurb for the back cover—she also graciously pointed out various small errors and inconsistencies.

A huge cadre of individuals helped whip this book into shape on relatively short notice. Thanks to Delories Dunn de Ayuso, Jill Gómez, Sarah Fraser, Rick Sacks, and John Giles for proofreading. My daughter, Hannah Weighart, also proofread this book. Not yet 13, she is now mulling a future in covering the Terriers.

Any errors that somehow managed to slip by everyone are purely my own responsibility.

I also must thank many others who have helped me as a sportswriter. Terrier superfan/historian Sean Pickett began posting my modest game recaps on his website back in the 1990s. Subsequently, I must express my gratitude to everyone I have worked with over the years at US College Hockey Online. Thanks especially to all of the USCHO writers who gave me permission to quote them in this book; I have named them where appropriate in the text. I also must thank Dave Hendrickson in particular for his support and advice over the years. Thanks also to Dan Shaughnessy of *The Boston Globe* for permission to quote one of his great lines in this book.

Those interested in learning more about the life of Spanish conquistador Hernán Cortés should start by reading *Conquest: Cortés, Montezuma, and the Fall of Old Mexico* by historian Hugh Thomas, published by Simon & Schuster in 1995. As far as I can tell, this is the definitive biography of Cortés. If you want to know the full and historically accurate legend behind the "Burn The Boats" theme, start with that tome.

Lastly, my wife, Ellie, handled all of the desktop publishing as usual while also stretching her skills by creating the layout for the 16-page photo spread. I would not be able to produce any of my books without a great team effort on the home front.

Scott Weighart
September 2009

INTRODUCTION

How did they do it?

Trailing 3-1 with one minute left to play in the biggest game of their lives, the Boston University Terriers pulled off the most dramatic successful comeback in the history of college hockey's national championship final, tying the game 3-3 with 17.4 seconds remaining before winning it in overtime.

It was not only BU's fifth national championship.

It was a game for the ages.

Whatever the future holds for this remarkable group of players and coaches, the story of a magical night in our nation's capitol will be retold for decades to come. Yet there is so much more to the story beyond the thrilling finale.

The Terriers won more than just the sport's biggest prize during the 2008-09 season. Due to an unusual alignment of the planets with regard to scheduling, this particular year happened to present the program with the opportunity of winning a total of seven different titles.

BU won all seven championships. They kicked off the year by winning the season-opening Ice Breaker tournament on home ice, one of very few opportunities to win early-season hardware. Like many teams, they competed in a holiday tournament, and they won the Denver Cup in enemy territory.

Come February, only four teams in the nation have the chance to win a title of any sort. A trademark of the BU program is its domination of the Beanpot tournament, held on the first two Mondays of February for the unofficial bragging rights among the Division I schools in the immediate metropolitan area of Boston. As they so often do, BU won the Beanpot in front of a huge crowd at the TD Banknorth Garden in Boston.

After trailing the emerging Northeastern University Huskies in the Hockey East standings for months, BU capitalized when their Huntington Avenue counterparts stumbled during their final regular-season game. The Terriers beat Providence on the season's last day to clinch the league's regular-season championship.

Next, the Terriers successively ousted Maine, Boston College, and UMass Lowell to win the Hockey East tournament—arguably the most difficult league championship to win in college hockey. None of it was easy, but the outcome was a fifth trophy.

From there, it was on to the national tournament. Underdogs uprooted all of the top seeds except BU. In the Northeast Regional up in Manchester, New Hampshire, the Terriers blew out Ohio State before great goaltending and some lucky bounces helped them eke out a last-minute win over the University of New Hampshire in its home state. That Regional Championship gave BU a sixth title, sending the team to the Frozen Four in Washington, D.C. It was the program's first Frozen Four since 1997.

Two fabulous wins later, BU claimed its seventh title in a comeback for the ages against Miami University.

So when I raise the question of how they managed to do it, the real question is, how did the Terriers do all of *that*?

If you're looking for a quick sound bite in response, you've come to the wrong place. I attended 28 of the Terriers' 45 games and saw or listened to almost all of the rest of them on the television, computer, or radio. I interviewed the head coach and his three primary assistants as well as about half of the team at great length several weeks after the season ended. With all of that material in hand, I pulled together the book you're about to read. There were quite a few defining and determining minutes from the offseason, preseason, and the season itself, and many are described here for the first time.

In the end, though, I found no easy answer to how BU managed to come through in every single high-stakes game they played all season. The fact that this success story must include a historical account of a Spanish conquistador attempting to conquer Mexico nearly half a millennium ago says something about how far one needs to go to try to make sense of it all.

Some of the big wins were routs, but most were cliffhangers. Somehow, some way, the Terriers emerged with a trophy whenever there was one to be held. I have to conclude that the success is due to a recipe that would be impossible to specify. The ingredients included talent, senior leadership, chemistry, and coaching but also some degree of good luck. As you will see, the good fortune was sometimes off the ice as well as in the heat of the battles.

If there is a common denominator in all of this, though, it might be that BU as a program had become fed up with being good enough—tired of winning no more than a Beanpot, if that. The players and coaches emphasized their determination to raise the bar in every aspect of how they approached this season.

So how high did that bar get raised? Terrier coach Jack Parker believes that this was the best team in Boston University's storied history thus far. Likewise, it is tempting to try to gauge where the team stands in the ranks of college hockey's all-time great teams. However, I think it is impossible to compare teams of different eras. This year's BU team did not blow out teams in the way that the Terrier champions did, and their record is not close to the stunning 30-2-0 mark that BU's 1978 champs held or to the far more astonishing 42-1-2 record of Maine in the 1992-93 season. Led by Paul Kariya and Jim Montgomery as well as two future NHL goalies in Garth Snow and Mike Dunham, Maine apparently won *eight* titles that season.

I would be hard pressed to say that this BU team had a better year than that, but I think that their record and achievements are arguably comparable… and while I am by no means an expert historian of the sport, I can't think of any other team that had a comparable year in terms of winning so many high-stakes games.

My point is that college hockey has changed. As this season's national tournament showed, there is far more parity of programs across the board. A last-place team in Hockey East beating a first-place team is only mildly surprising now, whereas anything other than a blowout in similar circumstances 15 years ago would be an accomplishment for the underdog. Technically, goaltenders have made dramatic strides, and double-digit blowouts are a rarity these days. Additionally, almost no team has the opportunity to earn more than five or six titles in a season.

In the end, I think it will be a long time before anyone has a strong argument as to whether they can top BU's 2008-09 team as the best of this young century. If a team is both lucky and good enough to equal or better a seven-championship season, then I will have to doff my visor-free helmet to them. If a program is able to tie up a national championship game with two or more goals in less than 59.5 seconds—and go on to win in overtime— then we will have to acknowledge that the Terriers' legendary comeback has been outdone.

Until then, I now ask you to travel back in time. Our story will begin on a low note with BU losing in the Hockey East semifinals to bring the disappointing 2007-08 season to a sorry end, and it will continue through many hard-earned wins, culminating in the numerous celebrations that followed that amazing victory in Washington, D.C. The book has been broken down into five sections intended to appeal to the college hockey fanatic:

- The PRE-GAME SKATE covers all of the key events that shaped the championship team during the offseason and preseason.

- The FIRST PERIOD reviews the action on and off the ice during the fall semester, a time when games are more spread out over the first three months of the season.

- The SECOND PERIOD features all of the highly-concentrated schedule during the rest of the regular season, running from early January through March 8.

- The THIRD PERIOD describes the Terriers' run through the various postseason tournaments, starting with the Hockey East playoffs and continuing through the excitement of the NCAA Regionals and the Frozen Four.

- The OVERTIME attempts to capture the many celebrations that followed the national championship while also serving as an epilogue to the story.

After all of that, you should be able to reach your own conclusions as to how BU managed to have such an amazing run of championships. As you read about the exploits of captains Matt Gilroy, John McCarthy, and Brian Strait along with their many teammates, you will learn how this team truly adopted a theme derived from the exploits of a different sort of captain, Hernán Cortés. "Burn The Boats" could have been no more than a catchy slogan on a T-shirt. Instead, the theme morphed into something very real, a spirit of never giving in or giving up in the face of adversity or in favor of taking the easier way out.

In fact, it seems fitting that to write the phrase "Burn The Boats," you must start with "BU."

PRE-GAME SKATE

Preseason: March through September 2008

MIDNIGHT STRIKES ONE HOUR LATE

The clock struck midnight one hour late for Boston University's 2007-08 season. At exactly 1 a.m., the final buzzer sounded. In a game that had started at 10:40 p.m. due to a triple-overtime battle between Boston College and the University of New Hampshire in the other Hockey East semifinal, Vermont dealt with the delay much better than BU. The Terriers had raised hopes of qualifying for the national tournament by going on a characteristic 11-2-0 run in the homestretch, only to revert to many bad habits and unfortunate tendencies when they self-destructed at the TD Banknorth Garden with a 3-1 loss to the Catamounts. In the wee small hours of the morning, the team had nothing else to do but mull the disappointment.

"Quiet, very quiet," Terrier defenseman Brian Strait recalls of that locker room. "Especially with that many seniors. It's tough being a guy who goes to BU thinking, 'Oh, we're going to make the NCAA tournament every year' and not being able to do that. It's a tough pill to swallow. We weren't shocked because of how we'd played that whole season. It wasn't 'How could we have lost this game?' We weren't that great of a team. We were an average team last year. So was Vermont. The better average won."

"It was certainly a tough atmosphere in there," says Colin Wilson of the last game of his freshman year, which also threatened to be his final collegiate game, period, given that he was expected to be a very high pick in the NHL draft in just a few months. "Everybody was down. I personally was wondering if it was going to be my last game in a BU jersey."

The Boston University hockey program has been characterized by winning big games almost every year. While national championships and league titles are obviously the most impressive achievements, it's perhaps even more striking how the team has managed to come away with at least one major accomplishment even in years that otherwise were major disappointments.

The 1998-99 Terriers exemplified that theme. That team finished with a dismal 14-20-3 record, but somehow they morphed into a latter-day Montreal Canadiens for the legendary Beanpot tournament. Behind great goaltending and incredibly purposeful team play, they won the February classic—for the fifth of six years in a row! The 2003-04 campaign was another off year, as the Terriers barely made the eight-team league playoffs by pulling out a last-minute victory over the University of New Hampshire. Yet BU salvaged some satisfaction when they stunned top-seeded archrival Boston College by winning the best-of-three quarterfinal series in the Eagles' home rink.

In fact, looking at Boston University's NCAA tournament appearances and Beanpot championships over the last few decades, the number of seasons that they failed to accomplish either goal can be counted on one hand.

Unfortunately, 2007-08 was one of those years. Although the team was not remotely among the worst BU teams ever, it was one of the more disappointing teams in recent memory. Yes, the team had lost a Hobey Baker finalist in goaltender John Curry, but returning goalies Karson Gillespie and Brett Bennett had performed well in limited duty. Otherwise, the team had lost only a few top scorers to graduation, and some highly touted recruits were coming in to offset those losses.

As a result, Terriers fans were stunned when the team got off to an 0-4-1 start. Although a stirring win over Cornell in front of 18,200 fans at sold-out Madison Square Garden gave some hope, that victory would turn out to be the unhappily premature high point of the season. The team proceeded to bottom out when they followed up that effort by getting swept decisively by archrival BC and then reaching a woeful 4-10-2 record on December 7.

Although the goaltenders were the scapegoats in the eyes of some, this was really a team effort in an ironic sense of the phrase. The coaching staff admitted that they had treated the season-opening series out in Anchorage, Alaska, as a pair of exhibition games, and the result was a loss to the fledgling program of Robert Morris University, followed by a tie with Alaska Anchorage. Subsequently, the team struggled to have all cylinders firing together on any given night.

A year earlier, I had written a feature story about the position of goaltender. Terrier coach Jack Parker emphatically believes that the position of hockey goaltender has evolved more dramatically than any other position in sports over the last few decades. With better coaching and conditioning—as well as bigger goalies and larger equipment—it has generally become harder to score goals. It used to be that a save percentage of 88-90 percent was quite good, but that was many years ago. In my January 2007 article, I had quoted Parker as saying "These days, if your team doesn't have a .920 save percentage, then *your team sucks."* A year later, Parker suffered through watching his own netminders post a .878 save percentage for the year.

In some games, the skaters played their hearts out—only to have the goaltending negate huge advantages in shots and scoring chances for the Terriers. On other nights, however, the goaltenders played very well, only to have the skaters do little or nothing in front of them. On a hockey team, 12 forwards, six defensemen, and one goalie typically play on a given night. Somehow, this team made 12 + 6 + 1 add up to something like 15 or 16 for most of the fall semester. A great team can make 19 players feel like 22 or more.

More disturbingly, the team's psyche was just not reflective of the great BU teams of the better part of the last 20 years. Covering the team for US College Hockey Online—as I have for about a decade—my sense was that the Terriers were annoyed at teams that played hard against them. BU would go up by one goal and then play as if hoping that the slim lead would be enough. The players seemed to expect that wins would just happen, and the vibe I got early in the season was that they viewed their disappointing stretch as something that had happened to them rather than something they *made* happen. Thus inconsistent goaltending, a lack of synergy, a lack of killer instinct proved to be the formula for mediocrity.

"I think you pretty much nailed it," BU forward Brandon Yip says after hearing me attempt to capture the shortcomings of the 2007-08 Terriers. "I think a lot of people blamed it on goaltending, but that's just one part of our game. Last year, just like you said, we were really inconsistent. We'd have one or two lines show up one night; the next night those two lines would disappear and the other two would show up. In this league, you can't do that. You've got to have four lines and six D going every night."

For the team's legendary coach, the season-ending loss epitomized everything that had been wrong for much of the season. "That single game was just what happened to us all year," Parker says. "We were almost good enough and satisfied with being not quite good enough. 'It's okay to be okay.' And I didn't think we got good goaltending in that game, which is another example of something that happened all year long. We didn't battle hard enough, we didn't play hard enough, and we didn't get good goaltending when we needed it. All of that added up to another loss, and that loss was the nail in the coffin.

"It was a major disappointment. Not just that loss: It wasn't just that we lost in the semifinals of the Hockey East tournament; it was that we had left ourselves in a situation where we had no way to get into the national tournament unless we won Hockey East. We had a real solid second half but not enough to overcome what we did in the first half. And, in reality, we never beat a real good team."

The frustration only mounted a few weeks later, when archrival Boston College won the national championship. But what if the Terriers had done somewhat better during the 2007-08 season? What if, say, they had won the Beanpot as well as the season series with BC? If they had done those two things—or maybe even one of those two—they probably would have qualified for the national tournament, and people would say it was another pretty good year.

But would that have changed the program's hell-bent intensity when it came to ensuring that the bar was raised dramatically for the subsequent season? In general, the seniors believe that the disappointment fueled their intensity but that a better showing the previous year would not have made them less determined for their final year.

"If we won the Beanpot and made the NCAA tournament, it would have been a pretty good year," winger Jason Lawrence concedes. "But I don't know that it would have changed the mindset of this team. I think that the guys we had this year were ready to do something great. Obviously, seeing BC win the national championship and receive all the accolades they got lit a little more of a fire under us, but I think this year the mindset was right when the guys came in."

"That was the worst," defenseman Matt Gilroy says, reflecting on the BC title. "That really helped us. Seeing BC get to throw out the pitch at Fenway Park and take part in all of those things was really hard to take."

"Last year we came out thinking that just because we had BU on our chests that we were supposed to win games—that we were supposed to be given these things," adds Lawrence. "In retrospect, it wasn't that way at all, and we suffered for it. This year we knew that we were going to have to earn everything we would get."

So everyone connected to the program—coaches, players, and fans—was getting restless after another year in which the team had failed to reach real heights. Now *two* recent national championships had ended up out at The Heights in Chestnut Hill—Boston College won it all in 2001 as well as 2008—while BU had not even appeared in the Frozen Four since 1997. While BU has built an astonishing legacy in the Beanpot, any program would trade a half-dozen Beanpot titles or more for one national championship.

The program had two heartbreaking near misses in NCAA Regional Championships—losing in overtime to UNH in 1998 as well as in an epic quadruple-overtime game ("It wasn't even hockey after awhile," recalls Parker, referring to the collective exhaustion of the players) against St. Lawrence, with Rick DiPietro in the BU net, in 2000—but that was as close as BU would come to college hockey's biggest stage in a 12-year span.

Terrier Nation was getting restless. In our increasingly blog-centric world, some fans on the US College Hockey

Online message board at www.uscho.com started suggesting that Parker's best coaching days were behind him. One writer for *The Daily Free Press*, BU's student newspaper, echoed this sentiment. Despite winning two national championships and leading the team to 22 NCAA tournament appearances, 20 Beanpot titles, six Hockey East championships, and 12 final four berths—there was a definite vibe of "what have you done for us lately"— especially among younger fans.

Parker barely noticed such chatter. At age 63 and with 781 wins under his belt, the "Godfather of BU Hockey" (as Bernie Corbett, the radio voice of BU hockey, likes to call him) could shrug off the ravings of some disgruntled fans and student journalists. He is the kind of coach who makes life easy for a journalist, as he is unbelievably candid and transparent. I've read articles in which BU sports psychologist Len Zaichkowsky describes Parker as a "reactor," and that resonates with me. Whatever you throw at him, he will come right back at you with a quick, honest reaction or perhaps an even faster quip. If he thinks you're off the mark by praising his team, for example, he will make sure that you know that he is not buying into your opinion. Not infrequently, he will be calm and relatively pleased when the team does everything right but loses… or agitated when his squad plays carelessly but wins in spite of themselves.

On the heels of this disappointing campaign, the real challenge was to respond to the toughest critic of all— himself. "I have always had doubt. If we lose three games in a row, I have doubt. I've always been worried about the game passing me by or people not listening to me or not being able to adapt to the younger generation. But it has never been triggered by a fan's opinion of our team, ever. I hate to tell the *Free Press* or the Internet people, but I've never read any of that stuff in my life.

"There were people grumbling in the eighties over the exact same thing," Parker adds, alluding to a three-year stretch starting in 1986-87 when the program posted a so-so record of 19-15-3 followed by years in which the final totals were 14-17-3 and 14-21-1... before proceeding to make the final four in seven of the next eight seasons. "I've always said that it's a real simple thing. If we get good players, we can coach them. If we don't get good players, we can coach them to get better but not to get good enough. So our situation has always been marked by how good we are at recruiting, and this rink has made it a lot easier to recruit."

Agganis Arena, opened in January 2005, holds more than 6,300 fans, and the steep pitch of the stairs ensure that no seat is more than about 60 feet from the ice surface. Perhaps even more significant for recruiting, however, the players' facilities are first-rate—superior to many professional clubhouses and probably surpassed only by the University of North Dakota's astonishing Ralph Engelstad Arena on the collegiate level. The rink unquestionably drew more talent, but the best season of the Agganis era to date had been 2005-06, when the team won its first Hockey East championship since 1997. The first-rate facilities had not ended the Frozen Four drought, which, as of April 2008, had reached 11 years and counting.

A GOALIE-GO-ROUND

In Parker's view, the team's shortcomings were all too obvious. "Not doing well last year, I wasn't thinking 'Maybe we've lost it as coaches. Maybe I should step down.' None of that stuff entered into it because I knew what our problem was. Our problem was very simple: Once we solved it, things changed around here. It had nothing to do with coaches or facilities or anything but recruiting."

Some players have told me that Coach Parker is the kind of guy who starts worrying about the next season immediately after the last game—even if the team wins the national championship. However, even that turns out to be an understatement. Parker and his staff had been reflecting on the team's personnel deficiencies for months and talking about how to improve the team's fortunes for the 2008-09 season as far as back as late 2007.

In particular, the team's goaltending was a hot topic among the coaching staff. Senior Karson Gillespie would be graduating, so the team had given a scholarship to Alberta native Kieran Millan back in February 2007. The question was whether that would be sufficient to address the team's concerns about netminding. Sophomore Brett Bennett was the heir apparent in goal, but he had proven to be erratic at best once the job was his. The team went through a goalie-go-round in which Bennett, Gillespie, and freshman Adam Kraus all got a crack at the job, but a real solution never materialized.

"After the first half of the year, we knew we weren't in the situation we wanted to be in," Parker says. "We had Kieran Millan coming in, so the question was 'Should we have Kieran and Bennett here, or should we have Kieran and somebody else?'" Given how crucial it is for any team to feel good about its goaltending situation, it was possible that the team would make the unorthodox move of having *three* goaltenders on scholarship. The staff had been tracking Grant Rollheiser from British Columbia, and he committed to BU in late February 2008.

"The final decision wasn't made until the end of the year," says Parker. "We decided to bring in two freshmen and start all over." Bennett was cut from the team. Given the alternatives of keeping his scholarship at BU or going back to juniors before completing his two years of college eligibility elsewhere, he opted for the latter.

It came as a surprise to the players. "We thought that [Parker] would just take time away from him next year— get one of the new kids in, make him the starter," recalls Brian Strait, Bennett's roommate at the time. "You never really think he's going to tell him that he's not going to be on the team. It was a shock to all of us. He was pretty shocked, too, but he's a good kid. Afterward he went up to Coach to thank him for the opportunity. I'm glad that it's worked out for him—he's going to Wisconsin next year. Obviously he just needed a different path. It worked out for him, and obviously it worked out for us."

The move also came as quite a surprise to Kieran Millan, hearing about all of this from afar in Canada. "When I committed, John Curry was the goalie, and Brett Bennett and Karson Gillespie were waiting in the wings. From what I'd heard, Brett was a really good goaltender. I thought Bennett would be the starter with me coming in as a freshman; I'd have to pay my dues for a couple of years. I didn't expect them to release him from the team, but it happened. I didn't really understand. It surprised me a bit, but I saw it as an opportunity for myself."

Meanwhile, Parker certainly didn't feel that this one move would be sufficient. "Then the other problem was 'What else is wrong? It isn't just goaltending. We can't just blame it on *that* guy. It's the other guys; it's us. It's a total team effort.'"

Yet further decisions to address the bigger picture were clouded by uncertainty surrounding two of the team's most talented players. Star defenseman Matt Gilroy had declined several NHL offers after his sophomore season, and it looked highly probable that he would go pro now that his junior year had just ended. Likewise, everyone knew that freshman forward Colin Wilson would go very high in the NHL Draft in June. His decision would have to be postponed until he saw where he was drafted in June, so the coaching staff had no idea whether or not he would return.

SKATING BACKWARDS WITH MATT GILROY

Gilroy's story has to be one of the greatest stories of figurative rags to literal riches in the history of the college hockey. As a defenseman spends a considerable amount of time skating backwards, it is appropriate to devote some space here to skating backwards in time to consider Gilroy's story.

Unlike most BU players, Gilroy was not a hot recruit who had NHL scouts drooling or even intrigued when he was playing in high school and juniors. At age 18, Matt was not shaving. He was 5-7 and just 145 pounds, a late-blooming victim of "Irish genes," according to his father, Frank Gilroy.

As Parker has often reminded everyone, he did more than fail to recruit Gilroy: He told him not to come to BU. However, Boston University had a huge pull for Gilroy and his family. His father was a star basketball player at St. John's from 1977-1981. Earlier in the 1970s, Billy Schaeffer—father of former Terrier defenseman Kevin Schaeffer—was another standout for St. John's before going on to play with the red, white, and blue ball in the American Basketball Association for a few seasons. The future Terrier dad also shared a high school alma mater in Holy Cross of Flushing, New York with Dennis Wolff, who would go on to coach the BU men's basketball team from 1994 through 2009.

"The reason Schaeffer came here was because Mr. Schaeffer found out through our basketball coach that we were trustworthy people," Parker says. "Even though he wasn't getting a scholarship he'd have a chance to get a scholarship once he made the club, and that's exactly what happened to him. The Gilroys recognized that it worked out great for the Schaeffers, and they knew them. They were thinking it worked out great for them, so it would be a good spot for their kid. Obviously, it worked out even better.

"But I think the major reason he had a big interest in BU and big interest in pushing his way onto the club was that he knew when he arrived here that he'd be treated fairly, and sooner or later he might have a chance to get a scholarship because that's what happened to Schaeffer."

Gilroy had played forward in juniors, but the team had enough right-shooting forwards lined up for what would be Gilroy's freshman season. Parker told him he would have to play defense—probably as the seventh or eighth defenseman on the team initially. Again, Gilroy was not deterred. He had played defense back in high school and figured he could do so again. He came to BU, but he did have a request. He wanted to wear No. 97.

Parker is a traditionalist who disdains the idea that college players should wear Gretzky-esque high-digit numbers. However, he previously made an exception with goalie Jason Tapp, who wore the unorthodox No. 83 as a tribute to his physically disabled sister. Likewise, there was a compelling reason to make an exception this time around. Gilroy wanted to wear the number in honor of his brother, Timmy, who died in a bike accident in 1993, a few weeks after Matt's ninth birthday. Timmy was just eight years old at the time.

Playing youth hockey together, the boys had coveted Gretzky's No. 99 but had to settle for 97 and 98. Matt originally wore 98 but switched after Timmy's passing as a tribute to his brother. Now he would continue the tradition as a Terrier.

The coaches and players realized that Gilroy could play as soon as he started practicing, but he didn't crack the lineup until he got an opportunity to play in an early-season exhibition game against the U.S. National Under-18 Team. As usual, I covered that game for USCHO, and Gilroy more than held his own against a talented lineup, including future NHL star Patrick Kane. From that point on, Gilroy played in every game of his college career except for one instance when he was a healthy scratch as a freshman.

As much as Gilroy wowed me with his obvious offensive talent from the get-go, his seriousness and intensity made an even greater impression. He carried a sense of gravity about him; he could be described as somber, even, in press conferences. In addition to wearing No. 97, he would come into those post-game sessions wearing the pale blue shirt that he always wore under his jersey, matching his eyes. The shirt had a small logo on one side reading "Timothy Gilroy Memorial Summer League" with the logo of a basketball player in the middle. Gilroy had two of the shirts and told me that equipment manager Mike DiMella patched them "a thousand times" before there was no choice but to retire the shirts prior to his senior season.

For quite a while, though, it appeared that there would be no senior season for Gilroy. After a promising freshman year, Gilroy's stock rocketed during his sophomore year thanks to nine goals and 17 assists for 26 points in 39 games. He earned recognition as a second-team All-American and a first-team All-Star in Hockey East. At the very least, NHL scouts could envision him as a valuable power-play defenseman in the big league. Gilroy discussed his professional offers with Parker and decided to return for his junior year.

At the time, Parker told the Long Island native to consider himself a senior going into junior year, as it was so probable that he would go pro after his junior year. In February 2008, his youngest brother, Kevin, committed to the Terriers, but that seemed unlikely to prevent Matt's early departure. Gilroy also would be forgoing the opportunity to be the team's co-captain, but his focus still remained on leaving the team.

Shortly after the disappointing loss to Vermont, Gilroy believed that going pro was inevitable. "I thought it was going to happen," Gilroy says. He visited several NHL teams, including his hometown New York Islanders as well as New Jersey, Florida, and Tampa Bay. Then everything hit the fan at the Gilroy household the night before a scheduled meeting with Parker. "The night before we met with Coach, I was at home with my sisters, my mom, and my brothers, and they were ripping me apart: 'How could you *do* this? Look at it!'

"That's when we put it all down on paper with being captain, my brother coming, graduation, and getting a final shot at it. Those four years, you can never have back. I was about to go visit Chicago, and my dad was footing the bill for this just in case I decided to come back to school so I didn't lose any eligibility. My family advisors, my dad, and I went into Coach's office to talk about it. After that meeting, when I was done hearing everyone's words, I was like, 'I'm going back to school.' We got out and I said, 'Dad, I'm going to call Chicago and cancel the trip.' The next day I went to Coach and said, 'I'm coming back; I don't want to do this anymore.'"

Obviously, that was great news for Terrier nation, but unfortunately sore feelings erupted due to miscommunication. Parker believed that he had been extremely clear about the fact that he fully intended to give away Gilroy's scholarship, given that it was such a foregone conclusion that Gilroy would go pro. Additionally, the team needed to use that scholarship to lock up another recruit before he committed elsewhere.

"There was never any question about whether that was going to happen in *my* mind," Parker says about the pulled scholarship. "In fact, when he came and told us that he was thinking of coming back and then that he wanted to come back in two different conversations, I said, 'Number one, you shouldn't come back; you're ready to play in the NHL, and, number two, I've already given your scholarship away.' And his father said, 'We're not worried about that right now.'"

Although he didn't say so to the Gilroys at the time, Parker actually wasn't too worried about it either. While Colin Wilson was several weeks away from the NHL Draft and thus unable to begin to make a decision, the coach believed that Wilson very likely would sign with whatever NHL team drafted him. Parker then could give Wilson's money to Gilroy. In the meantime, though,

Parker believed that Gilroy was okay with the fact that his scholarship was pulled—that is, until Bennett opted to give up his scholarship and go elsewhere.

"In his mind, he thought he had gotten his reservations about leaving across to me many times, so there was a communication gap between he and I about what was going to happen at the end of his junior year," Parker says now. "I should've told him 'By the way, you're not getting Benny's money, either. Benny's money has got to go to a goalie, not you.' So there were a lot of hard feelings about that. Matt felt bad that his dad was going to have to pay [for his senior year at BU]."

CAPTAINS COURAGEOUS

With Gilroy back in the fold, he assumed the role of co-captain as soon as the offseason began along with forward John McCarthy. The pairing appeared to be nicely complementary beyond the obvious contrast of having a defenseman with a forward. Whereas Gilroy characterizes himself as the "real serious guy, older, more competitive," McCarthy is less hot-tempered and not quite as deadly serious. "We call him 'The All-American Kid'," Gilroy says, though McCarthy shook his head and rolled his eyes at that description. Still, you can see it. A native of Andover, Massachusetts, McCarthy is tall, friendly, classy, and upbeat, and he was the quarterback and captain of his football team back at St. John's Prep, leading his squad to the state-wide Super Bowl.

Unlike Gilroy, McCarthy had not enjoyed much of the limelight through his first three years as a Terrier. In fact, any fan who mistakenly equated scoring with leadership probably was surprised at his selection as a co-captain. McCarthy had mustered just eight goals and eight assists in 109 collegiate games played.

Yet those who closely watched the team respected the fact that he had embraced his role and given it his all. "When I came in, I was fighting to get in the lineup,

21

and the most familiar thing to me was killing penalties, winning faceoffs, and playing a fourth-line role. I thought that would be the quickest way to get in the lineup, so that's what I did, and I ended up playing that role for three years."

Even as a freshman, McCarthy was often the forward of choice when killing a five-on-three power play. A fixture on penalty kills, he proved to be a good face-off artist and defensive specialist. More importantly, people around the program took note of his character. "What struck me getting to know John McCarthy and his family over the last few years was that we had a pretty special guy," broadcaster Bernie Corbett says. "Let alone anything about hockey, this was a guy who was a cut above.... There were questions about Gilroy and Wilson returning, but I knew from the get-go that we had a good guy in John McCarthy."

As he does with most Terrier captains, Corbett got to know McCarthy during the offseason. "We've got the right guy here," Corbett remembers telling his broadcast partner, another former Terrier co-captain, Tom Ryan. "We've got a guy who understands the tradition and the legacy of what BU hockey is all about. He knows that recently we haven't lived up to the expectations of our program and our legacy, and it's been compounded by what's been going on down the street over the last decade."

Junior Brian Strait rounded out the team's leadership as the assistant captain. Like McCarthy, Strait's contributions to the team had been less obvious to the casual observer. Along with Eric Gryba, Strait would be one of the two defensive defenseman on a team rife with blueliners who had visions of sugarplums dancing in their heads in the form of goals and assists.

Strait also served as a foil to Gilroy as his defensive partner, minding the store in his own end while liberating Gilroy to be creative on the attack. He had been the

captain of the U.S. Under-18 team, leading that team
to a gold medal in the 2006 Under-18 international
championship in Sweden. Like Gilroy, he has more of the
serious warrior personality. Muscular and incredibly fit,
he had struck me as unusually mature from day one at
BU—right down to his perennial five o'clock shadow.

With their tenure of leadership in its early days, the
captains had no idea how quickly they were to become
ensconced in a controversy with their coach. With the
goaltending situation addressed and Gilroy's status
resolved, albeit with some hurt feelings, the team still had
to address other shortcomings. "We had made a decision
that one of the problems we had was that we didn't have
enough BU hockey players," Parker says. "We had a lot of
guys who had the uniform on, but they weren't guys that
we would refer to as BU hockey players. They weren't
serious enough or determined enough to get in the lineup
or working hard enough. They were happy to be okay."

After some reflection, Parker determined that rising
senior Steve Smolinsky and rising junior Zach Cohen were
the poster children for these deficiencies. "Those two
guys fit that to a T, and we wanted to purge the team of
guys that didn't want to pay a price," Parker remembers.
"They were completely different in their lack of paying a
price. Smolinsky was a laid-back, I-don't-want-to-rock-
the boat kind of guy, and Cohen was just lazy, I thought.
So why should I keep those guys who are setting a bad
example? I had made up my mind that not only was the
goalie going but that these two guys were going, too."

To the average Terrier fan, cutting the two players
would have raised a few eyebrows, but it would not
have been a shock. While Smolinsky and Cohen both
had showed some potential, neither had contributed
too much to date. The small, speedy Smolinsky was
popular with teammates, who sometimes joshed him by
making race-car noises as he sped around the ice during
practice. Yet he had scored all of three points in his first

three seasons, and he only cracked the lineup three times as a junior—his smallest total of all three years at a time he might have hoped to break through for more playing time. "Obviously, my career hadn't panned out the way I wanted to," Smolinsky admits. "It was hard for me the first three years because I was always afraid of making a mistake and to be myself. I knew that if I got a chance and messed up, then that could hurt me. I think that made it appear to Coach that I wasn't working as hard."

For Zach Cohen, it had been a somewhat different story. Like Smolinsky, he was a well-liked player. Eric Gryba told me that Cohen has more nicknames than anyone on the team. The most frequent was Ziti, but Chris Higgins in particular always seemed to have a bizarre nickname of the week for the Illinois native: The Great Zitini, Cleveland Zitowski, and so on. Cohen had played in 33 games as a freshman and obviously had size and skill, but his skating appeared to need work, and he was rarely a factor on the ice. He scored a bit more as a sophomore but played a lot less, as the coaching staff gave ice time to those who had worked harder for it in practice.

"I thought it was going to be pretty easy to come here and accomplish everything I wanted to," Cohen says. "I didn't have the work ethic that I needed to have to be able to perform here. The end of my sophomore year at my year-end meeting, Coach talked to me and said he wasn't sure what he was going to do [in terms of keeping Cohen on the team]. You're not expecting that to happen."

As a courtesy, Parker invited the captains-elect to his office to inform them of the decision. Parker's office is upstairs at Agganis Arena, and it is impressive, a little intimidating—significantly larger than some studio apartments that I lived in during my graduate school days. A row of trophies could be seen on a shelf high above Parker's desk on the far end of the office. Closer to the door, there's an area with comfortable chairs and couches—clad in scarlet upholstery, naturally—around a table. It's an ideal spot for chatting with an incoming recruit who has already been wowed by the waiting area with all of its trophies and paraphernalia, including a book of hockey cards depicting former Terriers who have made it to the NHL.

In this case, though, the meeting revolved around who might go rather than who might come. Strait recalls the conversation. "Coach came to us and goes, 'I don't think I'm going to have them on the team. I'm going to tell them both to leave.' And we were really shocked. You told Brett to get out of here, and now you're going to tell two more guys?

"Right before he was about to do it—the day that he was going to bring them into his office to tell them—we told them, 'Don't go to his office.' We went in and said, 'Don't kick these guys off the team.' And he was pissed at us: 'Why should I listen to you? What have *they* done?' And we said, 'They're way more valuable to this team than you can believe. You're not in the locker room every day; you don't understand what it's like. Those guys are good kids, and they're better hockey players than they've displayed. They can be a big asset to this team. Don't kick 'em off; you're gonna regret it.'

"And you know what? After he heard that, he said, 'I'm going to take some more time…' But we knew leaving there that it was going to be okay."

That's not exactly how Parker remembers it. "I wasn't angry. The captains-elect came in and said, 'You're making a big mistake. We want these guys on the team.' And I said, 'Yeah, why? Because they're friends of yours? Because they're good guys? I know they're good guys: They're great guys. Just because they're good guys we should keep them on the team? They don't do what we want them to do. They never have, and why would they now?' I listened to them. I said, 'You've got your suggestions—I don't agree with them. I'm staying the way I am; they're going.'"

According to Parker, he didn't seriously reconsider his decision until the next day, when Matt Gilroy returned to his office with a display of fervor. "The next day Matt comes in, almost adamant, and goes, 'You can't *do* this. I'm not going to *let* you do this.' I said, 'Matt, you're the captain; you're not the coach. You don't have any say in this. You had your suggestion, and I appreciate it.'

"He said, 'Coach, you can't do it!' He kept hammering on it. 'I *guarantee* you I'll make these guys work hard!' And the only reason I took them back was that the captains in general and Matt in particular were adamant about this. Why get in a pissing contest with the most important guys on the team—and the guy who's already pissed off that I took his scholarship away? So the next time we met I told them, 'Okay, we'll keep them, but they're under *your* wing.' I told them, 'They could be gone by October 15 but right now they're here.'"

As events would prove in the season to come, it would turn out to be a great decision for all parties. The captains had scored some points by sticking up for two popular teammates and winning them an 11th-hour stay of execution—although Parker told both players exactly what had transpired and that they had been granted a "reprieve" as opposed to "carte blanche."

"Those guys weren't a cancer," Gilroy says. "Maybe they weren't playing up to their potential at that point, but they're two guys who are great team guys in the locker room. Especially Smo: If you go down the line, 25 of 27 guys on the team would say that he's the best teammate. Those two guys came back, and look what they did for us down the run. It was unbelievable. That was the first time we acted as captains."

Although this was a victory for Gilroy as a leader, it must be regarded as a highly ironic one. Both Cohen and Smolinsky were scholarship players. Had they been cut from the team, Parker believes that Smolinsky would not have left—he would have used his scholarship to complete his education at BU, given that he had only one year to go. However, Zach Cohen probably would have transferred to enjoy his two remaining years of eligibility… and *that* money could have been given to Gilroy.

"WE JUST WON THE OFFSEASON!"

The next offseason moment of truth for the program came in June in the form of the NHL Draft. Unlike Gilroy, Colin Wilson had been pegged as a star from a young age. His father, Carey Wilson, scored 427 points over an NHL career that spanned ten seasons with the Calgary Flames, Hartford Whalers, and New York Rangers. A dual citizen—born in Connecticut during his father's playing days but raised in Winnipeg, Manitoba—Colin had starred as a AAA Midget player before joining the U.S. National Team Developmental Program, playing for the Under-17 and Under-18 teams. It certainly was a recruiting coup for BU to bring him into the program.

On the ice as a Terrier freshman—not quite 18 years of age when the season began—Wilson had a good year, posting 12-23-35 scoring totals in 37 games to solidify his status as a top draft pick. Ultimately, he would be drafted seventh overall in the first round by the Nashville Predators. Off the ice, though, the year proved to be somewhat of a struggle for the budding star.

It can be a mixed blessing when a team recruits players from the U.S. Under-18 team. Obviously, the team always features extremely talented players, and being part of the team gives those players an opportunity to go through an unbelievably rigorous conditioning program, as well as a full season of playing against college hockey teams, prior to beginning a college career of their own. However, big talents sometimes come packaged with massive egos.

"One of the things we were concerned about was whether some guys from the National Development Program were going to lose some of their selfishness

27

and play more for the team," Parker says. "In Wilson's freshman year, he really struggled with his teammates. He was just so worried about what's going to happen to *him*. 'Where am I going to wind up in the draft? Am I going to make the junior team? Am I going to be drafted high?' So he had a really hard time with that—he was immature about it."

"It's definitely different coming in from the U.S. National Team," Wilson says. "You haven't played juniors yet; you don't know what seniority is. I had played with kids from my same age group all my life, and all of a sudden I'm a 17 year-old playing on a team with a 25 year-old—[senior goalie Karson] Gillespie—last year. So that was a totally different experience."

However, fellow freshman Kevin Shattenkirk—a former U.S. Under-18 team player himself and a very mature rookie—made Parker aware that there were mitigating factors to be considered. "You've got to cut him a little slack," Shattenkirk told his coach. "When we were on the Under-18 Team together, he was on a team where everybody on the team, all year long, all they did was talk about the draft —except him, because it wasn't his year to be drafted. Now he comes to this team and everybody has either already been drafted or they're going to be a free agent. No one's getting drafted except him. That's all he wants to talk about because that's all we talked about last year."

Wilson admits that the draft and the prospect of suiting up for Team USA for the World Junior Championships in January affected his focus on playing for BU as a freshman, though he also feels that he was an easy target for criticism. "I think it was definitely a distraction. For anybody who's gone through the draft as a college player, you're playing college and you're wondering if you're going to be a good college hockey player and if you're going to keep up your draft status. It definitely was a distraction, but at the same time it was a little tougher in the dressing room because everybody knew that was going on for me, so it was very easy for people to say, 'Oh, you're just worrying about A and B instead of C.' It definitely made for a tougher freshman year."

If the team had been playing well, Wilson's focus on the draft might have been the subject of some good-nature ribbing and sarcasm. With the team struggling below .500, though, the veterans had little patience with the young freshman's subject of choice.

Parker was frustrated with Wilson's inability to adjust. "Wilson didn't get it. He couldn't help himself—to the point where I wasn't going to have *him* back either. I told him so and told his family advisor and his father in June. It was after the draft. I told his advisor, 'Look, I think you should advise him to go pro. He doesn't fit in here; he didn't have a good time here. He's too worried about himself. People would think I'm nuts to want to get rid of the seventh pick overall in the NHL, but he could be a bigger deterrent in the dressing room this year than he was last year. If he doesn't want to change—and I don't think he can—then I don't want him on the club. His best interest may be to move on.'"

So another offseason irony had emerged. Although the reasons were very different than they were with Gilroy, Parker now had urged *two* of his most talented players to leave. Wilson's family advisor asked the coach if he told Colin all of this and suggested that Parker share his perspective with Colin and his father. By that point, Parker's patience had almost run out with Wilson, as weeks had gone by since the June draft without any inkling of a decision.

"It was 50/50 as soon as the season ended," Wilson recalls. "If anything, me leaving was a little more probable because I wanted to be a pro hockey player. Everybody does, especially growing up in Canada. That's the goal, and I want to get there as quickly as possible. So I was excited about that, but a lot of it had to do with whether the team who drafted me wanted me to leave. I ended up going to the Nashville Predators, and they were pretty laid back. They said, 'Hey, if you want to go back to school, go back to school. We'd love to sign you and watch you develop, and we'd prefer that. But if you want to go back to BU, we fully support it.' So they were great with that.

"I kind of knew I wanted to go back to BU within a few days of the draft [because of a sense of] unfinished business, and at the same time I really do like college and I thought it would be better for my development. It was a chance to get to be more mature on the ice and off the ice, which I definitely accomplished."

The problem was that Wilson had not made a clear indication to Parker that his stance had evolved from leaning toward going to very likely staying. Eventually, Parker got fed up with Wilson's apparent failure to make up his mind. "He's dragged it a long time after the draft whether he's coming back or not. So I told him that 'My best assessment is that you ought to get out of here. You should sign a pro contract. It will be best for you, and it'll probably be best for us, and here's why. You don't do this well or that well, and you're too worried about this or that, and you're still hemming and hawing. Nothing's good enough for you: You don't want to come to BU, and you don't want to sign with Nashville because they want you to play in the American Hockey League, and *that's* not good enough for you either.'

"He said, 'Hey, Coach, first of all, at no time did I think I was not going to come back. I know I've dragged this out, but two days after I got drafted, you could ask Shatty or [Colby] Cohen: I called them and told them I was coming back. I want to come back. As far as the other thing is concerned, I know I made a lot of mistakes last year. But when you recruited me, you recruited me because you thought I was a good hockey player and a good kid, too.

"'Coach, I know I can be a good kid again.'"

That assertion seemed to mark a turning point for Wilson.

"Come on back," Parker told his young star, softening his tone dramatically. "No problem. But you're not going to tell *me* you're going to be a good kid: I never had a problem with you. But you've got to show your teammates—that's the most important thing. If you show them that, you'll be terrific for us. If you can't show them that, I might be telling you to go sign come December."

Wilson not only returned; Parker said that he absolutely proved to be true to his word. "He came back, and one of the best things that happened was that he made huge steps that way."

According to Gilroy, the team felt an immediate boost when Wilson announced that he definitely would return. "When he finally decided to come back, it was 'We just got better again.'" Bernie Corbett recalls thinking, "Well, we just won the offseason!"

BOYLE, TOIL, AND TROUBLE

As the summer months progressed, the freshmen recruits trickled in. Some players went home for a break and then returned for workouts. Meanwhile, the captains had decided on some initial small steps when it came to setting the right tone. "When a new recruit came in, everyone had to dress the same," Gilroy says, acknowledging that he came down on his brother as much as anybody on that front. "People would wear their draft stuff and their USA gear, and Straity and Johnny and the coaches and I were really sick of that. Everyone had to look the same and act the same. We wanted to be a team and start looking the part and acting the part."

The next sign that the bar was going to be raised significantly came when the players got an e-mail from the team's Strength and Conditioning Coach, Mike Boyle, who has earned an outstanding reputation for his work with the Boston Bruins as well as preparing football

31

players for the Scouting Combine leading up to the NFL Draft.

Boyle announced that all returning players would have to be able to beat test scores that were unprecedented in the program if they wanted to play. These included incredibly challenging times on a variety of tests, including a five-mile bike ride; two-mile run; shuttle run; and the "10/10" test. With the latter, the idea is to run on a treadmill at a pace of ten miles per hour while the treadmill is at a ten-percent grade. Depending on the player's weight, the idea was to be able to run at that level for as long as two full minutes.

While I am admittedly twice the age of these athletes, I am in good shape and couldn't resist trying the 10/10 on my own. For me, I would say that running at ten miles per hour—basically a six-minute mile—is not very difficult to do for two minutes. Walking briskly—say, at five miles per hour—on a ten-percent grade is also no problem. I can do that for a good 30 minutes, and it's a challenging but reasonable workout.

Doing both at the same time, though? That's intense. I would describe it as trying to run up a mountain road at something short of a sprint, except for the fact that the road is racing rapidly underneath as your feet struggle to keep pace. You are well aware that a painful face plant is a definite possibility if you don't wait too long before jumping off, so I found it quite harrowing in addition to being extremely taxing. Suffice to say that I bailed well before one minute, and even then my calves felt like jelly afterwards.

Trying again another day, I was able to get through two full minutes on a ten-percent grade at a speed of 7.5 miles per hour. It was not fun, but it gave me a much better idea of what it must be like to go two full minutes with the double challenge of speed and grade. As before, my calves felt wobbly pretty quickly, but I got through that. Around the one-minute mark, though, my whole

windpipe started to burn. The seconds felt like they
ticked by at about half-speed. During the last 30 seconds,
I felt foggy-headed, and my legs got very heavy, but I
managed to make it. Still, it took a good 20 minutes for
my throat to stop aching.

Obviously, Division I athletes are in much better shape
than I, but many Terriers were daunted by the challenge
upon receiving Boyle's e-mail. "It was like 'Oh, shit!
This is serious!'" Gilroy recalls. "Since I'd been here,
the test scores had never been that hard or that serious.
These were doable scores, but they were at the higher
level. Mike always wanted us to do that but he hadn't
demanded that we do that. He was like, 'This is it. If you
don't do it, you've got to do it again.'

"Guys are puking; guys are freaking out. Guys are
passing out from running. That's when you start
becoming a team, in those moments. Everyone was like
'Oh my God—how are we going to get through this?'
Everyone was kind of shocked until you put your mind to
it and say 'Look what I can do.'"

To be fair, the players varied in their opinions on how
challenging the various tests were. Brian Strait, for
one, was pleased about the higher standards and not
particularly daunted by the raised expectations regarding
conditioning—mainly because of what he had endured
while training for the U.S. Under-18 team out in Michigan.
"I told Matt and John before the season, 'We've got to
make the preseason a lot tougher than it's been.' When I
played out in Ann Arbor, it was hell every day before the
season. It was workouts four times a week, boxing twice
a week on top of that, then you were doing conditioning
and practice on top of that.

"You went home every day and all you wanted to do
was just go to bed—nothing else. I said, 'We've got plenty
of time to be well rested once the season starts, but we've
got to make it painful at the beginning of the year and see
if guys want to sacrifice a little bit.' Guys were calling me

before the testing saying 'What's up with this? This is ridiculous.' And I was like, this is not that difficult. I've done this before. If you just set your mind to what you can get done, it's not as hard as you think. It doesn't feel good, but it's not as hard as you think. They're saying 'Two minutes on the ten/ten—that's impossible!' It's not impossible: We all did it. When you don't have a goal, you don't do it—you jump off before."

The level of commitment also was quite a contrast to what Strait had experienced as a freshman and sophomore for the Terriers. "The past two years, it was playing a little shinny in the captains' practice, do some lifting, and get out of here. We were committed to have the start that we'd *never* had."

The testing also provided quite an introduction for the freshmen, although they were not required to perform at the levels dictated for the upperclassmen. "I'd never lifted weights before this season," Kieran Millan says. "When school was over, I would go to my cabin to swim and water ski, come back in two months, go to camp for a few weeks and try out for the team. I got here in the summer and was in really bad shape. All of the other freshmen had worked out before. I was just a kid who liked to play hockey but never took it as serious as them. I didn't pass a single test."

Even for the seniors, the testing was a major challenge, according to Chris Higgins. "For me, the 10/10 test was the toughest. Each year, you try to come in and beat your scores. Usually the best scores would be 1:30, 1:40— maybe two minutes at the most. It went by weight classes, but Boyle pretty much came in and said everybody had to hit two minutes. In years past, that had been about the best time. For my weight class—about 185—the best time had been about 1:40.

"We knew we had to put a whole 20 seconds on top of that. That was pretty nerve-wracking, but still every person hit that goal. When everyone hit those goals that

Boyle set for them, that's when we knew we had a serious team, a team of BU hockey players who wanted to give their very best every day."

A TEAM THEME

While the players strained to reach Mike Boyle's lofty goals, Parker sought ways in which the bar could be raised emotionally in addition to physically. When former assistant Ben Smith—best known for coaching the U.S. women's Olympic hockey team to a gold medal in 1998—visited Parker up at his home in Gloucester in early September, a motivational theme emerged. Smith showed Parker a story that he had printed out off the Internet. It was a motivational article about the exploits of Hernán Cortés, a Spanish explorer whose feats occurred almost 500 years ago.

In 1519, Cortés set sail from Cuba to Mexico. According to *Conquest: Cortés, Montezuma, and the Fall of Old Mexico* by historian Hugh Thomas, Cortés allegedly talked of winning "vast and wealthy lands" for the conquistadors, reaping kingdoms "greater than those of our monarchs." Most relevantly in light of the players vying to live up to Mike Boyle's testing regimen, Cortés also described "great rewards wrapped around great hardship."

The Spaniard's challenge would be to explore the interior of Mexico, colonize it, and plunder the fabled riches of gold that were said to be possessed by Montezuma II, Emperor of the Aztecs. Various obstacles threatened Cortés in accomplishing that goal. When he landed in the Yucatan Peninsula with 11 ships and 500 horses, mutiny loomed as a possibility. A significant faction of the soldiers did not want to march into Mexico's interior; they wanted to return to a cushy life in Cuba.

Cortés decided to quell the rumblings in dramatic fashion. As he explained after winning the 2009 national championship, Parker understood the events to have occurred as follows: "The last night before going inland to get the treasure, he gave one last order and that order was to burn the boats. His aides looked at him and said, 'What are you talking about?' 'Burn the boats: I want you to go out and burn the boats.' And they asked him why. He said, 'Because I want to raise the level of commitment. If you want to get this treasure, you have to raise the level of commitment because nobody else can do this.' His quote was: 'If we're going back, we're going back in *their* boats.'"

It's a great story. The Internet version that Parker read is not 100% accurate, though. According to Thomas's biography, Cortés never burned any boats at all, but he did order the destruction of all but one of the larger boats. Showing a little gamesmanship, perhaps, he claimed that the boats were unseaworthy due to an infestation by wood-beetles and needed to be destroyed. First, though, he removed all useful supplies from the boats. Over the centuries that followed, the poor handwriting of one scribe led to a misinterpretation about the burning, as the Spanish word for "burned" is quite similar to the word meaning "scuttled."

Cortés then told the men that if they wished to take the one remaining large boat back to Cuba, they were welcome to do so… but that he was confident that they would regret their decision because of the riches that were to be had when they reached the interior of Mexico. No one took him up on the offer. The sense is that some feared that his offer was merely a ruse—a way to root out the mutinous rebels—while others reflected on the fortunes that were there to be made if they went on the dangerous mission inland.

While Parker may have not had all the facts, there is absolutely no question that Cortés fully intended to raise the level of commitment of his troops and instill the attitude that retreat is not an option. His destruction of the fleet brought the rumblings of the cynics and defeatists among his men to an abrupt halt. Cortés and his men proved to be equal to the task of conquering Mexico, and

Cortés personally governed Mexico from 1521 to 1524, plundering a substantial amount of gold in the process.

So even if the Internet version of the story glossed over some facts, the core of the tale about destroying the boats in the name of eliminating doubt and conquering all is a stirring one.

The story immediately resonated with Parker—partly because he had happened to watch the movie *The Hunt for Red October* a week before that. No doubt borrowing from the Cortés legend, burning boats factored in that movie's plot as well. While reflecting on the story, Parker received the Cortés story again from another former assistant coach, Bobby Richardson, a few weeks later. Parker decided that this would be a theme for the 2008-09 Terriers.

With the ordeal of physical testing behind them, an ocean voyage factored into the next part of the story as well, though the port of call for this one was Gloucester, Massachusetts instead of Havana. The three captains joined Parker on his sailboat to talk about the forthcoming season—a tradition on the team. According to Gilroy, Parker talked about what he expected from them. The captains accepted this but also pushed back and told the coach that they had expectations of the coaches as well. "We just wanted everything to be equal, for everyone to be accountable—not matter who you were, where you were from, who's drafted," Gilroy says. "It didn't matter. We wanted to be a team. That's what the coaches were saying to us, too. I think that the players and coaches were on the same page this year, and that really made a big difference."

HATE THAT DIRTY WATER

On the heels of that voyage, the captains decided to bring back twice-a-week river runs. "Those suck, and you've got to get through them as a team," Gilroy says. "The closest we got as a team was in those situations where you have to say 'Shut your mouth and get it done.' That's what the river run was for: get up, get it done, go back to bed, go to class, and getting guys closer and closer. They were horrible."

At 6:00 on every Tuesday and Thursday morning throughout the preseason in September and early October, everyone on the team who was physically able had to be in the weight room at Agganis Arena, dressed and ready to run. Those who had injuries had to do a 15 or 20-mile bike ride instead. Defenseman Colby Cohen had an ankle injury, so he logged hundreds of bike miles over that five-week period.

Initially, the team simply ran down to the Myles Standish dorm in Kenmore Square and back to the Arena. Soon they built up to running down Commonwealth Avenue to the George Sherman Union before crossing the footbridge over Storrow Drive. They ran along the river before crossing it at the Massachusetts Avenue bridge before running along the north bank of the Charles and recrossing at the BU Bridge. They finished by running the several blocks uphill back to the rink.

It's not a particularly difficult run in and of itself, but the early hour combined with everything else the players had to do turned it into a hateful experience. Gilroy notes that hockey players are *not* runners by any stretch and immediately dismissed my suggestion that perhaps a few players enjoyed it. "Everyone *hated* it. It was the hour, plus then you had to go back to bed, get up, go to class, and still go to skate in the afternoon. But the best thing was that everyone was doing it, everyone was miserable together."

Admittedly soft from his dearth of conditioning, freshman Millan struggled through the runs but gratefully accepted the encouragement of Luke Popko, the fourth-line centerman who is one of the team's real worker bees. "Obviously, I tailed off," Millan remembers. "I think the first time I realized how good a team we were was on those runs. Popko would stay back and run with me—pushed me, got me in shape. It's something I never thanked him for but something you appreciate. That's what made our team successful this year: Everybody enjoyed being with each other, and everybody did what it took to make each other better."

HEADS UP

Those efforts continued in the video room. Right before the season started, the captains put together a lengthy PowerPoint slideshow with the help of the coaches. The team congregated in the video room just outside of the locker room's entrance at Agganis, and the players collectively reflected for a good hour and a half or two hours on what it means to be a BU hockey player.

"Everything we did this year just got everyone focused and mentally aware that we all wanted the same thing," Jason Lawrence says. "It put everyone's head in the right direction. It let everyone know that we meant business: It's not about what you want; it's what the team wants. The way everyone made each other accountable really raised the level of commitment."

For Lawrence, the atmosphere seemed reminiscent of the 2005-06 season, when Brad Zancanaro and David Van der Gulik reigned as co-captains, leading the team to its first Hockey East championship since 1997. "This year was similar to my freshman year with the accountability factor. If you slacked off, you knew that someone was going to get in your face because you were bringing the team down."

Building on the PowerPoint presentation, Parker decided to bring in some BU legends to reinforce the theme of what it means to be a BU player... and to be a national champion. From the 1978 national champions as well as the legendary 1980 U.S. Olympic hockey team, Jack O'Callahan gave a memorable speech. "O'Callahan told us about winning the national championship and told us that we'll remember these years for the rest of our lives," Higgins says. "He talked about coming back years later and how this is the best time of your life and how he wanted us to experience winning a national championship. That's when it really hit guys that this is what we're striving for, this is why we're here. It really stuck with us all season."

From the 1995 championship team, NHL stalwart Mike Grier shared his story about coming to BU as an overweight freshman and having to work his way into the lineup. "He talked about what it took off the ice—in the weight room, working hard every day, making the sacrifice—and about teamwork and camaraderie," says Higgins. "You don't have to like every guy on the team, but you have to respect them. When you put that jersey on, you have to go to battle with your other teammates."

Parker also showed the team a short but stirring mini-documentary about one of his heroes—Boston Celtics legend Bill Russell, who inspired Parker to wear No. 6 during his playing days as a Terrier—winning his last championship before retiring. Made by NBATV, the video is available on YouTube (as of this writing) by using the following search phrase: "1969 Russell's Final Championship."

The gist of it is how Russell possessed the unique ability to make his teammates better and how he led his team to one final championship over Wilt Chamberlain and the hugely favored Los Angeles Lakers in the NBA Finals. Before Game 7, Russell says that he told his teammates "There are a lot of things that have gone on but one thing that cannot go on. The Lakers cannot beat us. That's not something that can happen."

In so many words, that sentiment would prove to be extremely apt for the BU team in the 2008-09 season.

Bernie Corbett describes the decision to bring in various BU legends during the preseason—and ultimately throughout the year—as a "hanging curveball" just waiting for the coaches to hit it over the fence. Many of the players talked about how powerful and motivational these off-ice activities were in setting the tone for the team.

For his part, though, Parker downplays it all. "We've done that in the past," Parker says with a dismissive shrug. "In 1989, it was exactly the same situation: 'We've got to demand more of these guys.' Every year we tweak our approach as far as that goes. We could give ourselves credit in the way we approached the team or that some of the things in the preseason helped us get off to a better start, and certainly we changed our approach with team-building opportunities. We did more internal stuff this year instead of going outside.

"But frankly I truly believe that if we didn't have one guy talk to our team and we didn't show one Bill Russell highlight video, this team was made up of real good players with great leadership. When these seniors were freshmen, we had a struggling team for a while—under .500 the first semester—but we had two huge guys out of the lineup: [David] Van der Gulik and [Jekabs] Redlihs. When they came back, we went 19-0-1 and won the league tournament. We had the No. 1 team in the nation going into the tournament. So I still come down to this: We will be real good when we have real good players. You've got to have real good players."

TALENT SHOW

Motivational tactics aside, there was ample reason for optimism just in considering the pure talent on the team. Wilson appeared to be a lock to top his totals of nearly a point per game as a freshman, and Gilroy had dedicated himself to going out with his best year ever. Beyond them, the team had a strong senior class. At that point, Chris Higgins was the leading scorer of all active players in Hockey East, a great two-way player with excellent playmaking skills. Wilson would center a line with Higgins on his left wing and senior Jason Lawrence on

41

his right wing. Lawrence had been a solid contributor—averaging about 19 points per year—and seniors often finish with their best years.

The depth at forward didn't stop there. Brandon Yip, another senior and a right wing, had been Hockey East Rookie of the Year as a freshman, but injuries and some other distractions had kept him from fulfilling his potential since then. Sophomore Nick Bonino would center a second line with Yip on it, and assistant coach Mike Bavis would eventually tell me that Bonino was "about as skilled a guy as we've had in this league in 15 years." Bonino had shown flashes of brilliance early in his freshman year but scored just two goals in his first 14 games before finishing with ten goals in his last 17 games, so there was every indication he could break out. No one knew who would end up playing with that pair, but there were plenty of promising candidates among freshman recruits Chris Connolly, Vinny Saponari, and Corey Trivino, as well as McCarthy and a few other old and new options.

The defensive corps was enough to make any collegiate coach salivate. In addition to the excellent offense/defense pairing of Gilroy and Strait, Colby Cohen and Kevin Shattenkirk were another pairing in more ways than one. Shattenkirk was drafted 14th overall in the 2007 NHL Draft by the Colorado Avalanche, who then drafted Cohen 45th overall in the same draft. Both had shown incredible offensive skills but needed to be reminded to take care of business in front of their own net.

The third defensive pairing was another offense/defense combo—later to be a called a "Mutt and Jeff" duo by Parker because of their relative heights—in 5'7" freshman David Warsofsky with 6'4" junior Eric Gryba. Warsofsky would prove to be one of the most dazzling skaters and creative playmakers on the team, while Gryba had been somewhat inconsistent his first two years but definitely had the size and strength to provide the physical, defense-first glue in his own zone. All six had been either drafted or wooed to sign by NHL teams.

THE CRUELLEST MONTH

In "The Waste Land," poet T. S. Eliot referred to April as the "cruellest month." For Boston University hockey, September has been far worse. On September 11, 2001, former BU star Mark Bavis—twin brother of assistant coach Mike—had his life cut short because he happened to be on one of the planes that was hijacked by terrorists and flown into the World Trade Center.

In September 2008, amidst all of the efforts to pull all of the talent into a cohesive team, the program suffered two more great losses. After a battle with thyroid cancer, Meryl Starr Herman, co-chairman of the Friends of BU Hockey, died on September 17. In a eulogy, Parker praised her commitment to the program. For years, she had organized the team banquet among many other activities. The team decided to sell "Starr of the Game" bracelets in her memory at each home game to raise money for thyroid cancer research at Massachusetts General Hospital. By May, roughly $20,000 would be raised, and more than one person would raise the question of whether Meryl had a cosmic hand in pulling the team through its many close calls all through the championship season.

On September 29, tragedy struck the Terrier family once again. Former star goaltender Scott Cashman died of a heart-related condition at the age of 39 in Ontario. The netminder had played a key role in the program's reemergence as a national powerhouse from 1989 through 1993. The program decided to add a black patch with 'SC' in white letters on the left shoulders of the team's jerseys for the 2008-09 season.

BAKING AND BOILING

At the very beginning of the captains' practices that
kick off the on-ice activities during the fall semester, a
memorable scene unfolded at 2:30 sharp one afternoon
in Mike DiMella's equipment room. Freshmen Saponari,
Trivino, and Kevin Gilroy were on hand, and Saponari
and the younger Gilroy were getting their skates "baked."
Basically, the skates are heated up so they can be molded
to the feet for a better fit.

Suddenly, Matt Gilroy stormed into the room, his
temperature boiling over. His younger brother saw what
was coming. "As soon as I saw him coming in, I was
gone," Gilroy says. "I got out of there as fast as I could."

Kathi Brown, Administrative Coordinator for the hockey
program, happened to be there. As she recalls, Gilroy
walked in and just started yelling. "It's 2:30—you're
supposed to be at Boyle's!"

"Yeah, it's just 2:30 now…" Trivino said.

"What does Coach say?!" Gilroy replied. "If you're not
five minutes early, you're late!"

One of the players was still sitting on a counter. "Don't
disrespect Mike DiMella by sitting on his counter!" Gilroy
shouted. "Get the skates off—you're not wearing those
now—you're working out!!"

Then he turned back to Trivino, who was wearing
black. "You're not wearing the right workout clothes! It's
supposed to be red pants and a white T-shirt."

Trivino tried to explain. "Oh, I can't find…"

Gilroy cut him off. "Well, *go* in the locker room and get
'em on!!"

Kathi Brown recalls feeling dumbfounded. "I said to
myself, 'If something happens this year, this is the turning
point. I'm going to remember this moment for the rest of
my life.' I was just, 'Oh my God.'"

Kevin Gilroy typically received special treatment from
his brother—in reverse. "I probably got called out more
than anyone else," he remembers. "He was all over me

last year about doing the right thing—being on time, getting to class. I knew what I was getting myself into before I got here. It was good for me. It made me grow up a lot more and a lot faster."

NET GAIN OR LOSS?

With the leaders stepping up to get everyone on the same page, everything seemed to be shaping up for the coming season—with one enormous question mark. With many strong skaters returning, the only real anxiety about personnel revolved around the incoming freshman goalies. Everyone eagerly anticipated seeing the new guys between the pipes, and they weren't exactly wowed at first. Jason Lawrence experienced a flashback from his hometown of Saugus, Massachusetts. "When they first came in from the summer, we saw Kieran come out, and he just had these horrible pads and this horrible helmet. He looked like a goalie from a beer league up in Route 1 up at Hockeytown. We're shooting on him, and everything's going in."

Bernie Corbett heard the early goaltending reviews and began some serious wishful thinking, reflecting on former BU goalies from The True North Strong and Free who were outstanding in games but who had to be prodded to show much in practice, which is not an emphasis for most Canadian junior teams. "I started thinking of Michel Larocque and Sean Fields, who weren't exactly practice guys, and thought, 'That could mean nothing.'"

If Corbett reflects the eternal optimist, Gilroy was not as sanguine on the topic. "We were real worried about our goalies. When we first started skating, we were saying 'What's going on?' The upperclassmen are going crazy. We know what the preseason is, how we've got to get ready. The younger kids are just 'Oh, this is nice, hanging out with the guys, getting used to it.' The goalies were just that. They were young and just saying 'Whatever— let's get in the net and look at some pucks.' But they weren't saving anything. Everyone was worried about who was going to step up with the goaltending because every other piece seemed to be in place."

In retrospect, Gilroy realizes that there was too much of a rush to judge the new recruits. "It's tough to read because with a captains' skate there are tons of breakaways, tons of two-on-ones and three-on-ones, tons of shots. You kind of read into things too much. I remember being very worried, and I was totally wrong."

If the seniors needed to be kept away from their sharp objects and shoelaces during those initial practices, Millan was unfazed, predictably. He shrugged off the beer-league comment, telling me that he had figured he could scrape by with an odd-lot assortment of equipment until his BU gear arrived rather than shelling out money for something fancier.

Likewise, he hadn't fretted about the early practices— not out of indifference but because he knew he was coming off of a long break at the time. "Bringing in two freshman goaltenders, the upperclassmen are going to be nervous. I don't think either [Rollheiser or I] played great the first couple of practices. I know I basically hadn't been on the ice for two months. I had taken a lot of time off in the summer to have fun because I knew I wouldn't be home much for four years. I knew I'd have my chance to play and that I had five weeks to get in shape. So there was rust the first few practices, but eventually things started to progress."

Lawrence remembers feeling very relieved in short order. "Once he got acclimated, he started making saves and robbing guys who would usually put the puck in the net. I was sitting on the bench going, 'This kid might be on to something here.' He was."

DRESS REHEARSAL

At long last, after all of the anticipation, the team prepared to play an actual opponent. As usual, they played an exhibition game against a Canadian opponent—this time it was the Varsity Reds from the University of New Brunswick. It's always hard to gauge a team's performance against the Canadian schools, as the majority of the top young talent plays either Junior 'A' hockey or comes to the USA to play college hockey. However, the Terriers' 4-1 victory showed some promising signs. New Brunswick was the reigning champion in the Atlantic Conference, for one thing. Ultimately, the Varsity Reds would win their third University Cup—the biggest prize in Canadian college hockey—during the 2008-09 season.

Better still, the Terrier freshmen looked like they would contribute considerably. Chris Connolly played on the second line and scored the first goal of the game off of a good defensive play by Nick Bonino. Meanwhile, fellow freshman Vinny Saponari—whose older brother Victor was already a spare forward on the team—factored in two goals as well, scoring one while setting up freshman Corey Trivino for a nice snipe on another.

Freshman defenseman David Warsofsky looked short and slight but also wowed the fans with his electrifying skating ability. The two freshman goalies were seldom tested but seemed poised. Parker made clear that he had no fixed plan with the goalies. "I don't have any set idea that we're going to rotate guys or we're going to settle on a No. 1 guy right away," Parker said after the game, speaking to about four of us from the media. "Those who play well will be rewarded with further play, and both played very well today."

All systems appeared to be go for the start of the season. However, Parker revealed one more surprise shortly before the first game. He had read the "burn the boats" story to the team a few weeks earlier, and it had gone over well. "I thought it was great—a great story and attitude to live by," senior forward Brandon Yip recalls. "We're going the capture the gold—no excuses, no way out. It worked out great for us."

Now the players came in and found that the coaches had placed long-sleeved white shirts in their dressing stalls. On the front, it read "BURN THE BOATS" in scarlet lettering. On the back, there was a drawing of a large, overflowing pot of gold with D.C. written in scarlet on the black pot. This was an obvious reference to Washington, D.C., the site of the 2009 Frozen Four. Still, there were no instructions as to what the team should do with the shirts. "I remember getting here early and me and Strait were like, 'We're wearing them; these are our warm-up shirts for the rest of the year,'" Gilroy says. "I think it just reminded us what we were doing—seeing everyone in them was pretty cool."

Now Gilroy could feel good about retiring his pale blue Timothy Gilroy Memorial Summer League shirt in favor of this new shirt, emblazoned with a motto that the team would refuse to explain until after winning the national championship game over six months later. That theme would prove to be more appropriate than anyone on the team could have dared to hope.

FIRST PERIOD

Regular Season: Fall Semester

CRUSHED ICE

Team radio announcer Bernie Corbett had heard the story behind the "Burn The Boats" shirts, but Parker had made him shut off his tape recorder before telling him and then sworn him to secrecy on the topic. The motto impressed Corbett, but he knew that the words could prove to be no more than a catchy slogan. "It's one thing to talk the talk, but there's also the Bill Parcells view that you are what your record is," Corbett says. "So in the back of the mind, I thought that these guys are going to have to walk the walk this year." Despite winning the offseason, as he had put it, he still viewed the goaltending as the "big 800-pound gorilla in the corner of the room" that quietly made everyone in the program fret.

Finally, the team had the opportunity to begin to find out if they could walk that walk. As opening night approached, the team found that there were changes in the already impressive locker room. As always, the first thing that the players saw when they entered the capacious facility was a photo of former Terrier Travis

Roy, taken at a faceoff seconds before he crashed into the boards and ended up permanently paralyzed. That had happened in the first game after BU's last national championship. The opponent was North Dakota, and BU would face the Fighting Sioux in this season's opener as well—albeit with no banners to raise this time around.

Turning the corner, the players could see a new sign that had been the brainchild of assistant coach Mike Bavis. Under the heading of ARRIVE HERE, there was a list of puck-shaped bullets in front of five key points:

- WE CONTROL OUR ATTITUDE, WORK HABITS, & EFFORT

- LISTEN & FOCUS

- DO YOUR JOB

- NO EXCUSES

- IMPROVE

Someone also wrote the phrase "NO EXCUSES" on the white board in the players' lounge at the far end of the locker room, and it remained there all season. Given that the team had scheduled five of its first six games against highly ranked "brand-name" opponents in North Dakota, Michigan State, New Hampshire, Michigan and Vermont, there was no question that it would be easy to fall back on excuses if the upshot was, say, a 2-4-0 run in the early going. It would not take long to find out if there were any teeth behind the "failing to succeed is not an option" theme evoked by the "Burn The Boats" motto.

With so much riding on the goaltending, you might expect that freshman goalie Kieran Millan would be fraught with opening-night nerves. If so, you would be wrong, but no one knew it at the time. Parker had determined that there would be a moratorium on freshmen talking to the media, and he didn't lift it until second semester. This had never happened in my time of covering the team, and it was done quietly—several upperclassmen expressed surprise when I mentioned this to them in my postseason interviews—but undoubtedly the move had everything to do with having two freshman goalies who would be under the microscope given what had happened the previous season.

Whether or not the imposed vow of silence with the media helped, Millan felt no anxiety whatsoever—only a typically Canadian desire to get beyond practices and play some games that mattered. "The first game of the season, you'd assume that I'd be nervous, but I was just excited to be finally playing a game. We had a long training camp—in my old league we started games in the first week of September—so I just wanted to get it started."

Goalies are a notoriously eccentric breed. Former Terrier netminder Sean Fields refused to talk on game days, even when called on directly in classes. Denver coach George Gwozdecky once told me about a teammate who once vomited after eating a few small bites of a fast-food cheeseburger before a game—and then went out and earned a shutout. You guessed it: That goalie's new superstitious ritual before every single game was to eat two bites of a cheeseburger before throwing it up.

Even the less nutty goaltenders often go through some sort of pre-game ritual to increase their focus. Seeing teams get ready to take the ice below the stands, I often see netminders engaged in something akin to shadowboxing—shifting position, lunging with a blocker, flashing a glove, as if they are stopping an imaginary onslaught of Slovakian vulcanized rubber.

The soft-spoken, low-key Millan doesn't even do that. "I don't really have much of a routine. I eat with the team. Sometimes I feel like a nap between the pregame meal and coming to the rink; sometimes I'm not tired, so I don't have a nap. When I come to the rink, I don't do anything specific. I kind of stick to myself a bit, just sit quietly—just try to go out and stop the puck."

Ranked No. 9 in USCHO's preseason poll, Boston

University was the host of this season's Ice Breaker Invitational, which is hosted by a different program each season. There are only two or three season-opening tournaments with championships to be won, so this gave the Terriers one more opportunity to win hardware than they ordinarily would experience in a typical season. While the Beanpot, league championships, and the national tournament are always possibilities for the Terriers, they usually don't play for any sort of championship before the holiday tournaments around the New Year—and sometimes not even then. So this season marked an unusual opportunity to win seven titles, but naturally no one was mulling that remote possibility back in October.

In the opening game of the Ice Breaker, UMass dominated Michigan State with a 37-16 shot margin… only to lose by a 3-1 margin thanks to the heroics of diminutive Spartan goalie Jeff Lerg. That only made those close to the program wonder all the more how BU's goaltending would hold up.

Millan would not have to wait long to face some tests. The theme of the game's opening minutes was bend-but-don't-break for BU. With the exception of a good chance for Chris Higgins at 3:30, fifth-ranked North Dakota had the better of the opportunities early on. "I thought we played a good first eight to ten minutes," Sioux senior Brad Miller said after the game. "We didn't play very well after that. I can't remember any real positives after that…. Collectively, we weren't executing."

Meanwhile, buoyed by Millan's solid play when the Sioux had the upper hand, BU visibly gained confidence as the game wore on. Colin Wilson had a quasi-breakaway shorthanded, and freshman d-man David Warsofsky had a great rush punctuated by a slick move for a chance at 13:20.

Ultimately, BU took the lead during four-on-four play at 18:29. Nick Bonino got the puck off a Colby Cohen dump-in on the left-wing boards, and he raced toward the net before dishing to defensive partner Kevin Shattenkirk trailing the play for a wrister and the first of 177 Terrier goals for the season. No one could have guessed that those two ultimately would team up for goal #177 as well.

That set the stage for the offensive fireworks in period two. Just after a power play expired, North Dakota tied the game when Miller buried the rebound of a Joe Finley shot at the 21-second mark. BU countered almost immediately, as Wilson raced in on the left wing before hitting Lawrence at the far post for the easy tap-in.

With Agganis Arena public address announcer Jim Prior still trying to convey the details of the scoring of the previous two goals to the crowd, Bonino received a pass from behind the net and buried a wrist shot at the 59-second mark. Little did we know that it would be the first of 12 times that BU would score two goals in less than one minute over the course of the season.

"I don't think there's anything really harder in a game to do than to come back and score on the next shift after giving up a goal like they did — and they scored two goals," Miller said. "You've got to tip your hat to them. They acted like their goalie saved that one, and it was just a faceoff and they went back at it. Obviously it didn't faze them."

"That was the turning point," Parker said after the game. "They didn't have a chance to enjoy that goal and get back and put pressure on us. Before they knew it, it was 3-1, 38 seconds later."

Perhaps the most exciting aspect of the game was that the team continued to show a killer instinct instead of sitting on a two-goal lead—something we had seen very little of during the previous year's performances. The top line of Colin Wilson, Chris Higgins, and Jason Lawrence looked fabulous from the get-go and ended up together for almost every game of the season.

In particular, Wilson played exceptionally well on

opening night, scoring one goal, setting up another, and factoring in several near-misses. For an exclamation mark, Millan made a highlight-reel glove save to rob Matt Watkins halfway through the third period.

After the 5-1 victory, the players talked about the offseason focus and the newfound emphasis on "keeping the foot on the pedal," according to Shattenkirk. Yet they also knew that they had to grow beyond the tendency of the previous year's team, which often followed up a solid win with a disappointing loss. With No. 11 Michigan State looming, the Terriers had to be careful not to let up.

The result was a 2-1 BU win that was not nearly as close as the score indicated. In many ways, the game evoked memories of the previous night's game—except Michigan State received better goaltending from the acrobatic Lerg. "I thought our team was overmatched terribly," Michigan State Coach Rick Comley said. "We were okay for about the first half of the first period, and then we got three penalties that got them going. When they smelled blood, boy, they really cranked it up on us."

For this game, freshman Grant Rollheiser made his debut in net. The Spartans didn't test him, particularly, but he looked good. Meanwhile, freshman Kevin Gilroy played with his brother for the first time and almost scored on his first shift. However, BU struggled to solve Lerg. A Wilson shot trickled through the goalie and got pushed in by a teammate, only to have the referee rule that the net had been knocked off its moorings shortly before the puck crossed the line.

BU peppered Lerg with shots early in the second period, yielding a sole two-on-one break in return. Finally, while shorthanded, freshman defenseman David Warsofsky did all the heavy lifting on the first goal of the game, carrying the puck into the zone, losing it and getting it back. With two defenders on him, he couldn't get a shot off despite repeated efforts, but Chris Higgins finally snagged the puck and buried a 12-foot wrist shot for the overdue lead.

BU got what proved to be the game-winner at 14:57 of the period. Senior co-captain John McCarthy dug the puck out of the left-wing boards and fed it to Shattenkirk at the left point. The sophomore skated in, took a look, and fired a slapshot past Lerg for the 2-0 lead. Lerg kept it close, making seven or eight excellent saves, but the Terriers held on for the win. "Overall, it was a very good game," Parker added. "It's hard to pick out any one guy, although I thought Shattenkirk had a great game in all three zones. It was an unbelievable goal he got; he's got so much poise."

Winning the Ice Breaker trophy meant that the Terriers had already won more titles in two games than they had during the entire previous season. More surprisingly, it was the program's first 2-0 start in seven years. Yet the best omen of all had to be the fact that the goalies showed no obvious chinks in their armor, while the team played extremely consistent hockey.

"Last night for 60 minutes and tonight for probably 52 minutes we played very solid," Parker told the media. "I don't think we played that well off the bat for the first half of the first period, but after that we played extremely well, and I was very pleased with everybody's effort."

Although it was very early, it's hard to overstate how much these early successes mattered to the team. After all of the off-ice efforts to ramp up everyone's level of commitment, the team had taken advantage of the first opportunity to prove that all of the hard work and refocus would translate into W's.

"The biggest thing was the first weekend of the season," associate head coach David Quinn says. "On our team, there was a lot of anticipation of how our goalies were going to do. The team was concerned because of the summer and the fall. But when practices became real, and once that weekend happened, it put our guys at ease from a goaltending standpoint. At that point, our guys felt real good about our chances for the forthcoming season. I remember thinking after that weekend that we might have something here."

The players could sense it, too. "Everyone got along so well right away, and to beat North Dakota right away—a brand-name team—was huge," Colby Cohen says. "If we don't beat North Dakota, who knows where the direction of the season goes? We didn't get cocky; we were just very confident after that game and ran with it for a while. Right away, we were saying, 'We could be a really good team.' There definitely were some question marks surrounding the words 'Burn The Boats,' and I felt it all came together in those first games. We knew we had 43 more games to go, but it was just a very good start."

IRRESISTIBLE FORCES

The next challenge came in a very different form. After two games against ranked teams, BU next faced a league opponent in Merrimack. It was the perfect opportunity for the kind of letdown that had plagued the team throughout the previous season. The Warriors were coming off a 12-18-4 record and had been picked to finish dead last in the ten-team league according to the preseason coaches' poll. Yet they also have been a consistently hard-working team, and effort frequently trumps talent in college hockey.

When the puck dropped, though, it looked apparent that the Terriers had not taken the game for granted. BU took a 1-0 lead at 1:22. Corey Trivino carried the puck in on the right-wing side and flipped a backhanded pass to John McCarthy in the slot. The senior's shot appeared to be deflected, and Vinny Saponari buried the loose puck for his first collegiate goal. Then BU made it 2-0 on a power-play goal at 7:07. Gilroy fed it to Yip skating toward him from the left-wing face-off circle. Yip curled toward the net and fired a high wrister past Merrimack goalie Andrew Braithwaite.

Merrimack didn't get its first shot until 10:30. Still,

at times it felt like the irresistible force meeting the immovable object. The Warriors struggled to get any kind of attack going on but played valiantly when killing penalties, so Parker felt dissatisfied with his squad's special-teams performance—especially when Merrimack made it a 3-2 game—before BU's fourth line scored the backbreaker. Joe Pereira rushed the puck up the left wing for a shot, and Luke Popko knocked in the rebound. The final result was a 5-2 victory.

Perhaps the best news was that sophomore Nick Bonino was showing signs of breaking out offensively. He notched three assists for his second three-point night in just three games thus far. Six points in three games looked awfully good for the centerman.

Two days later, BU traveled to Durham to face the University of New Hampshire in a rare Sunday afternoon game. I listened to Bernie Corbett and Tom Ryan call the game on the radio, and it sounded like an early-season anomaly. Referees Tim Benedetto and Kevin Keenan called a total of 19 minor penalties, resulting in a whopping total of 17 power plays for the two teams.

When Corbett and Ryan reacted incredulously after the *opposition* was called for five consecutive penalties during a seven-minute span of the second period, I started thinking that the outcome of the game would not be terribly meaningful. The Terriers outshot the Wildcats 18-1 in that second period but still managed to lose a 2-1 decision.

Around this time, something interesting occurred during a practice. After earning a death-row reprieve the previous spring, winger Zach Cohen had managed to stay on the team, but that had not made one iota of difference in terms of ice time. "When I went home for the offseason, I just tried to rededicate myself to not taking a shift off— being more consistent and physical because we needed some bigger guys out there trying to hit," Cohen recalls. "You can't have Gryba doing all of it."

Despite his avowal to work harder, though, Cohen had made no headway with the coaching staff thus far. Cohen was a healthy scratch through the season's first four games while freshmen Andrew Glass and Kevin Gilroy, as well as sophomore Victor Saponari, earned auditions on the fourth line's left wing with Luke Popko and Joe Pereira holding steady as the center and right wing, respectively.

I asked Cohen if he felt that it was only a matter of time before he got in the lineup. "Not really," he recalls. "Coach told me that I wasn't as good as he wanted me to be. I thought I was playing well, but I wasn't playing up to what he thought. He didn't notice me enough out at practice. So I tried being physical and getting to the net."

Mike Bavis recalls a critical moment. "One thing that Coach used as a term this year is 'Attitude is everything.' It's not like we coached Cohen different this year. He decided he wanted to go in and prove people wrong. Quite honestly, he didn't even have that attitude at the start of the season. Something happened with him.

"During a practice, I can remember we played a small area game between the blue lines, and he absolutely ran over Kevin Shattenkirk on what Shatty thought was a late hit. Shatty wanted to fight him, almost. It was a turning point. He was less worried about being everybody's friend out there and more 'I'm going to earn a job here.' I think it was right around that time that Zach got his chance."

Cohen got in the lineup for the next game and proceeded to play in every game for the rest of the season. That next game was against yet another ranked opponent—No. 4, The University of Michigan, always loaded with talent and coached by the legendary Red Berenson. With BU ranked at No. 6, the matchup of heavyweights absolutely lived up to expectations in the early going, as the teams went at each other relentlessly for much of the first period. Once again, Millan's play early in the game proved critical... and easy to overlook in light of the final score.

"He's had a good learning curve," goalie coach Mike Geragosian says. "He's got a good *demeanor*. Use that word in your book. He's got the demeanor of a pro: quiet Canadian, a very educable kid, very positive."

BU had a good-looking power play minutes in, but then Greg Pateryn had an excellent chance to give Michigan the lead at 7:00, only to have Millan come up with a big save. Joe Pereira had an exciting chance for BU as a Wolverine power play expired at 11:00 , but then Michigan's Brian Lebler almost scored when the Terriers botched the puck handling behind their own net a few minutes later.

Finally BU took the lead at 15:01 when Kevin Gilroy backhanded home a fat rebound of a Nick Bonino shot from the left wing side. It was the freshman's first collegiate goal in just his second career game, as a knee sprain to Corey Trivino factored in Gilroy playing on the second line that night.

Michigan very nearly evened it up within 35 seconds, but Millan made a great kick save on Carl Hagelin. Michigan survived a five-on-three later in the period, but BU made it 2-0 before the second penalty expired. UM defenseman Eric Elmblad appeared to have the puck in front of him behind the goal line, but Terrier frosh Chris Connolly swooped around the net, stole the puck, and tucked it in past senior netminder Billy Sauer. It was Connolly's first collegiate goal as well.

That set the stage for another pivotal save by Millan, as associate head coach David Quinn recalls. "We go up 2-0, and 15 seconds later a guy walks out of the corner all alone—a huge defensive breakdown in the fifth game of the season—and he bails us out. It's one save, but it's a game-changing save, and he did that time and time again this year."

The 2-0 lead had not reflected the evenness of the game in the first period, but the same two-goal margin for the second period proved to be an entirely different matter. BU dominated play and capitalized again at 6:52. Colin Wilson made a great rush up the left-wing side before a quick succession of passes to Chris Higgins, back to Wilson, and over to Lawrence for the finisher and a three-goal load. "I can't fault our goalies," Berenson said. "A lot of their goals were tic-tac-toe plays. Our goalie would've absolutely had to stand on his head to make a difference on some of those shots."

At the final buzzer, the upshot was a resounding 7-2 victory. Parker expressed his satisfaction afterwards, reserving his highest praise for the team's performance in killing 10 of 12 Wolverine power plays. "The first thing that jumps into my mind is we were happy with our special teams tonight, and we were very happy with our goaltender [Kieran Millan] tonight," the Terrier coach said.

"I thought especially in the first period he had to make some tough saves and played very cool, calm, and collected. A bunch of guys played well. I thought Colin Wilson looked like an NHLer out there today, boy. But the best part of our game was how we killed penalties."

One year after starting the season with an 0-4-1 record, the team now owned a 4-1-0 mark. That improved to 5-1-0 the following weekend, when the team thumped the University of Vermont 7-2 up in Burlington. Colin Wilson scored two goals before the game was seven minutes old, and eight different Terriers had multi-point games that night.

The team let up briefly when the score was 3-1, but after UVM made it a one-goal game BU responded with four unanswered goals, starting with a Brandon Yip goal that proved to be the backbreaker. With the game already in hand at 5-2, Chris Higgins and Nick Bonino scored two goals in 49 seconds—the *second* time the team had scored two goals in under a minute during the young season—to round out the scoring in the waning minutes.

"They lit up Michigan for five on the power play last week and they certainly made us look like a Junior B team tonight," Vermont coach Kevin Sneddon told USCHO's Josh Appelbaum afterward. "I thought we made it so easy for them in front of our net compared to what we faced at the other end. They were tough, they were physical, strong on their sticks. We were the opposite."

That would not be the case the next time the two teams faced off, but for the moment, life was good for the BU hockey team, both on and off the ice. Driving back from Vermont, Parker noticed a small, defining moment. Parker sat near Terrier Sports Information Director Brian Kelley on the bus, and Colin Wilson approached Kelley on the trip home. "Hey," Wilson said. "It says on the scoresheet that I got an assist on the third goal. I wasn't even on the ice. I touched the puck but long before it was ever part of the goal. It's not only not my assist, it should be so-and-so's assist, so I'd like you to make that change when we get back."

Parker's eyebrows rose dramatically. "Wilson would've been looking for that assist a year before," Parker notes. "And I said, 'Hey Wilson, c'mere. You just made my night.' That was an example of how far he'd come."

TWENTY-SEVEN BROTHERS

Admittedly, strong performances on game days make life far more enjoyable the rest of the week, so that was a factor in the clubhouse culture that emerged early in the season. According to several players, the team evolved into a laid-back group of 27 brothers who sometimes quarreled but who generally really enjoyed being together each day. "Any time you're winning, everybody's happy and glad to come in here," Zach Cohen recalls. "Nobody was complaining about coming to practice. There wasn't a dreary silence."

On a typical non-game day, the players showed up at Agganis sometime between 1 p.m. and the start of practice, which usually began at 3. The usual routine would be to pick up one's laundry from the equipment room. Walking down the hallway, there were four large framed photographs of the BU championship teams from 1971, 1972, 1978, and 1995. Just before the entrance to the locker room, there was, noticeably, just enough room left on the wall to fit the portrait of one more championship team.

Then the players often would go through the locker-room entrance closest to the ice surface, just off the runway to the home bench. On the immediate left—after going by the Travis Roy poster and Bavis's reminders— there is the main locker room, perhaps 25 feet long and about 12 feet wide. The players' stalls for equipment and skates were there, and each stall had a ventilation system for whisking away the odors of sweaty gear. Beyond that was a smaller changing room with lockable lockers for street clothes and valuables. This was where the players change into their workout clothes. Going a little farther in, you would find a capacious bathroom on your left, including a Jacuzzi that must be at least five feet deep.

All of that said, the heart of the impressive clubhouse was the player's lounge, located on your left as you emerge from the bathroom—close to a second entrance to the locker room. Entering the lounge, there was a small kitchen on the right. Beyond that, there was a rectangular room with scarlet carpeting, a little over 20 feet long and 12 feet wide. It included the aforementioned white board, a table loaded with Terrier memorabilia in the process of being autographed, comfortable chairs and couches, a large flat-screen TV, and a ping pong table on the far end.

The team's Hockey East championship trophies were near the TV, while the walls feature photographic murals of former Terriers. The players could mull Chris Drury hoisting the Stanley Cup as a member of the Colorado Avalanche and Ryan Whitney posing with the Pittsburgh Penguins' intelligentsia at the NHL Draft.

Former captain Jacques Joubert was depicted holding the 1995 championship trophy, and the 1980 U.S. Olympic team—including four former Terriers in Jim Craig, Dave Silk, Jack O'Callahan, and Mike Eruzione—was featured as well. Rick DiPietro, Mike Grier, Tom Poti, and Keith Tkachuk were among the other Terrier greats on the walls. It was all enough to bedazzle a possible recruit or to evoke daydreams of glory in a current Terrier player.

In that 1-3 p.m. timeframe before practice, this was where the team really lived. Some of the players might be down the hall getting in their required daily workout in the enormous weight room, while others would opt to do so after practice. At any given moment, though, about two-thirds of the 27 players would be in this room before practice. Typically, a ping pong game might be going on, most frequently Nick Bonino and Brandon Yip battling it out for supremacy on the team. On the TV, the most typical fare is *NHL on the Fly*, a staple of the NHL Network, but *The O.C.* or the Game Show Network might make a sporadic appearance.

More than anything, though, this would be an opportunity for the players to enjoy each other's company, and that often involved chirping at each other. It might start with a story about what had happened with a given player the previous evening, and it would go off in any number of directions from there. The most common chirpers would be Yip, Higgins, Bonino, Vinny Saponari, Wilson, and Smolinsky, known for some great one-liners. However, any number of guys might get involved in the verbal swordplay.

Though just a freshman, Vinny Saponari—sometimes called "Napoleon Dynamite" because of his supposed resemblance to that movie character—proved he could dish it out as well as he could take it, often ragging on Gilroy because of his age. In turn, someone might bust on Saponari and other former members of the U.S. Under-18 team—sarcastically referring to them as the "chosen ones"

63

or something along those lines. Some of the freshmen
would catch heat for being airheads, and teammates
would ask them about when their spaceship would be
departing for galaxies unknown.

Co-captain McCarthy reflects facetiously on the lounge
scene. "Higgins is pretty funny; he wants to pursue a
career in modeling, I think. He definitely is the most
fashionable on the team. He wears a lot of hair gel and
designer clothes that a lot of us don't wear. He's all about
watching MTV and all the reality shows."

According to McCarthy, Yip earned the reputation of
being the most superstitious player on the team. "Before
the game, he always has to eat the same meal at T
Anthony's [the team's neighborhood restaurant of choice].
He orders spaghetti and chicken, so he thinks he's being
healthy by getting chicken but then he only eats the
spaghetti. So that doesn't work. He gives the same high-
fives to everybody when we're stretching. He tries to rub
everyone's stick blades on his so he can take their goals."

Yip also acknowledged that he was the biggest prankster
on the squad, though by no means the only one. "Yipper
was kind of a goofball, but once it was game time, he
would turn it on," Gilroy says. "He helped younger kids
realize that there's a time to goof around and a time not
to."

Eric Gryba and Gilroy would get competitive with the
teasing. "Gryba we always made fun of," Gilroy says.
"We called him the 'Alpha Male' because he always
thought he was the man, just like the big guy around
campus. Guys just love to give it to him." McCarthy
also added that Gryba sometimes was called "The
Lumberjack" because of his size as well as his love of
wearing flannel.

"It's funny because I give as much as I take, especially
from Matt," Gryba recalls. "I've made fun of Matt
ever since I came here, especially when he became an
All-American. I've been riding his case: 'Oh, the All-

American's talking; everyone shut up.' Or, 'Here's Hobey Gilroy. Let's everyone bow down.'"

If Parker was praising Gilroy in the locker room or wisecracking with him, Gryba could just catch Gilroy's eye and just *know* that Gilroy knew what Gryba was thinking: Coach's pet, Coach's boy.

"You have to be able to keep it light and to keep guys honest," Gryba says, all kidding aside. "You can't be screaming at guys every day, but you can say something to put a guy in his place. I'd be the first one to say that I need that sometimes."

The variety of personalities on the team became evident in that lounge—striking but perhaps not too surprising when you combine 27 young men who are anywhere from 18 to 24 years of age. You had quiet, relatively serious guys like freshmen Chris Connolly and David Warsofsky. Sophomore Kevin Shattenkirk was more laid back than a Gilroy or Strait but shared their maturity and leadership qualities. Speaking of laid back, the ultimate example would have to be fourth-line centerman Luke Popko. "Luke could be sleeping for four hours before a game and go out and do his job and be perfect," Gilroy says.

Unlike the previous season, Wilson found his sarcasm was readily embraced in the more laid-back atmosphere. He emerged as the tunemeister in the locker room, loading up his iPod with dance music for the clubhouse. "I think my biggest role on the team was bringing in techno to the locker room," Wilson says. "It's going to sound weird, but a lot of it was European techno that nobody had ever heard: Basshunter, Betty Vanasse, David Guetta." The seniors embraced it, and it helped Wilson find another role he could play as a good teammate off the ice.

All of that said, the biggest source of comic relief on the team had to be sophomore Joe Pereira, a small, energetic fourth-line forward who always did a good job of making himself a nuisance to the opposition on the ice, while

65

appearing to relish being the brunt of the jokes off the ice.

"We call him 'The Bulldog' because that's the way he plays—he's 100 miles per hour or nothing," McCarthy says. "He made up the nickname himself, which makes it even funnier. He's not too quick, so a lot of guys will tape something funny on his helmet, and he'll wear it all practice." At one point, Nick Bonino taped the word "Tool" onto Pereira's helmet, and the winger was mystified as to why everyone kept calling him that for a whole practice.

Pereira also would have to be called the team's official hypochondriac. "If he had a common cold, he could turn it into pneumonia, just like that," Gilroy recalls, chuckling. "He would worry about everything and be in a panic. He was always, 'I'm *so* banged up.' We'd say, 'Joey, you have a cold—get over it.' Everyone would give it to him on the team, but he loved it, and guys loved having him around."

"When he got out of the lineup this year, he made himself sick," McCarthy says. "He gave himself the flu somehow because he was so worked up and stressed out that he couldn't eat and couldn't hydrate—he literally *made* himself sick."

"He loves it," Gryba says of the chirps that Pereira received from the team. "He loves being there for the boys. He's the kind of the guy who is not the sharpest knife in the drawer, but he's a great kid." Gryba pauses to reflect and decides he'd better amend his comment about Pereira's intellect. "Actually, I don't know how much I can talk because he was named Academic Player of the Year for our team."

It wasn't unusual for Pereira to come in and find that someone had snipped the laces on his hockey skates, but, again, he seemed to enjoy it, and the antics kept the team's mood light. Veterans like Higgins and Yip proved to be exemplary when it came to demonstrating that you could be a nut or a character hanging out with the guys as long as you could turn on your game demeanor when the time came.

When the practice and conditioning as well as the ping pong and the verbal patter ended for the day, the players would leave the sanctity of the locker room, passing by another poster of reminders created before the season by Mike Bavis:

LEAVE HERE

- YOU REPRESENT BOSTON UNIVERSITY HOCKEY
- MANAGE YOUR TIME... GO TO CLASS
- DON'T LISTEN TO THE NOISE
- OUR BUSINESS IS OUR BUSINESS
- THINK TWICE... ACT ONCE

COACH CLASS

While the players' lives revolve around the voluminous locker room downstairs, Parker and his coaches spend the majority of time in their office suite on the upper level. Parker acknowledges that his approach to managing his players has evolved dramatically over the years. "Oh, absolutely. Kids are different now."

To illustrate how he has changed, Parker told me a story. One night several years ago, he had to turn over his team to an assistant coach due to the implantation of a heart stent. With that device in place, it could have been problematic if he had been struck by a puck on the bench. Not wanting to freeze in the stands at Merrimack, he opted to go to dinner with former player Travis Roy, who asked him about his 25 years of coaching up to that time. "Have a lot of things changed?" Roy asked.

"Not really," Parker replied. "The facemask ruined the game in 1980, and the kids are different. Everything else is the same."

"The kids have changed?" Roy asked. "Are they better now?"

"I don't think they're better; they're just different,"
Parker replied. Yet Roy's question reminded the coach of
an incident from 1979.

Terrier Jack O'Callahan was the captain of BU's team
and also of the East team in the senior all-star game.
Legendary Yale coach Tim Taylor had been charged with
running that team, and one day he walked into the locker
room to find his players "laughing like hell" only to go
dead silent when Taylor came in. Finally O'Callahan
told him the truth—a Yale player had been doing a really
good impression of Taylor. Taylor asked if O'Callahan
could do an impression of Parker. "Oh yeah, I sure can!"
O'Callahan said. With that, O'Callahan got up, walked out
of the dressing room, walked back in, slammed the door
behind him, and said, "You guys SUCK!"

"So that's how you were perceived back then?" I say.

"No, that's how I *was*," Parker says. "And then in the
Eighties, I realized it wasn't working." Around 1985-86,
then Terrier co-captain Chris Matchett made an "ass play"
to turn the puck over. Parker proceeded to ream him out.
"What the hell are you thinking for Chrissake?"

Well acquainted with Parker's rantings, Matchett
shrugged off the tirade… but the same couldn't be said for
the younger players on the team. "We couldn't complete
a pass the rest of the game, we were so uptight."

Assistant coach Ben Smith came to him and said "You've
got to stop this. You're intimidating the hell out of these
kids." Parker realized that "you can't coach out of fear."
He also believed he was fortunate enough to be open
minded and to listen to the good advice. He began to
change in favor of a more psychological approach in
which ice time—or lack thereof—would be the ultimate
reward or punishment for good or bad behavior.

"He used to be an absolute lunatic," Terrier alumnus
and Olympic legend Mike Eruzione told *Sports Illustrated*
in 1998. "He would yell and scream and turn different
shades of purple. Today he's much calmer and more of a

friend or father figure to the players."

It would be an exaggeration to say that Parker has become a mellow coach. He still yells at times—I remember Steve Smolinsky receiving a stern tongue-lashing in the runway behind the bench after a brutal turnover a few years ago—and he is absolutely blunt in his appraisal of his team. Still, it's fair to say that he has embraced a style that is much more low key than it once was.

In recent years—with over 35 years under his belt as the BU coach—Parker was fully prepared to trust players who had earned it. "It wasn't like the inmates are running the asylum," Parker says of the championship team's seniors. "They had proven from the first month [of the offseason] that they were mature, more into it, more focused, and more 'we want this for us' not just for me. It was a lot easier to coach 'the right way' when you gave them responsibility and they took the bull by the horns and did it well. It's a lot easier to have a good team when you've got the right senior leadership and the chemistry's correct in the locker room."

While Parker is quite right in crediting his seniors for their leadership and locker room chemistry, though, assistant coach Mike Bavis believes that it is all too easy to underrate Parker's role in manning the helm this season. "With the most talented team in the country this year, people would not realize how hard he had to coach with all the personalities on the team," Bavis says. "We had good kids—don't get me wrong. We had an older kid in Gilroy, younger stars in Shattenkirk and [Colby] Cohen, Nick Bonino, Colin Wilson as a top pick, etcetera. He really had to manage that and be on top of that whenever he sensed some negative energy. Coach did a masterful job of working with those guys, airing the dirty laundry."

As we will see, that would prove critical come February.

Bavis also praises Parker's intuition as to giving a player what he needs, when he needs it. "I think that one of his greatest strengths as a coach is his instinct on how to deal with guys individually—when to pull a guy in and say 'I love ya, and you're a great player,' and when to say 'you're supposed to be a great player, and you're not getting it done' and give him a kick in the ass, or when to sit him out to give him that message in a way that words never will. He's really got a sense of when the player is just not good enough and when he's not getting the message."

Parker's demeanor behind the bench is often revealing. One of my favorite memories of Parker comes from a December game against Boston College at Walter Brown Arena in the mid-1990s. Trailing by a goal with about 1:30 remaining, Parker pulled the goalie for the offensive-end zone faceoff. Within seconds, forward Mike Sylvia buried the equalizer, and the players reacted jubilantly while the crowd responded with the greatest eruption of cheers and leaps imaginable in a first-semester game.

Amidst the bedlam, though, I watched Parker's reaction. He merely turned around and strolled away in the other direction with his hands behind his back, idly looking at the ground as if deciding whether he should bother to pick up a dropped penny.

That's quite typical. You often will see Parker clapping heartily when the rest of the arena is close to silent, while he is more poker faced on the heels of a dazzling goal or brilliant save. "First of all, regarding the reaction: Good coaches shout praise and whisper criticism. You always get positive feedback [from the crowd] on a goal and negative feedback on a goal against. It's a good idea for guys to know that you appreciate their effort, so not only they know it, but everybody else knows it—especially when it's the little things like blocking a shot or a great effort on a defensive backcheck."

Consistent with that philosophy, skaters are awarded paw-print decals for their helmets—but only for doing the little things well, such as making a great defensive play, showing exceptional persistence on a penalty kill, or crunching an opponent with the best hit of the night.

FROM TOP TO BOTTOM

The Terriers probably didn't earn many paw prints in their next game, but they still emerged victorious due to one of the wilder finishes of the regular season. Playing up at Lowell, BU spotted the River Hawks a 3-1 lead, and it could have been much worse if not for more fabulous play by Millan all night.

Lowell still led 3-2 going into the third period when the going got weird. The River Hawks had to pull starting goalie Carter Hutton due to an injury, and that helped the visitors explode. Vinny Saponari tied it up at 9:13, only to have Colin Wilson cough up a bad turnover that led to a Mike Potacco goal, putting BU behind 4-3 with just over five minutes left. But in this tale of two cities in Boston and Lowell, it turned out to be the best of games and worst of games for Wilson. With 2:14 left, Wilson headed in an odd-man rush, passing to Jason Lawrence, who made a perfect cross to Chris Higgins to tie it.

Then, with overtime looming, Wilson got the puck in the left-wing face-off circle and buried a shot high on the blocker side to take the lead with just 15 seconds left. For good measure, Higgins scored yet again with six-tenths of a second remaining to make it an improbable 6-4 final.

That would be the third instance of two goals in under a minute as well as a harbinger of more late-game rallies to come. "I think that was the beginning," Wilson says. "We had a ton of tight games where we found the way throughout the season. People started going, 'Wow, we do have a lot of firepower on the team. We can get things done in the last couple of minutes.'"

"Being down two goals to a team like Lowell that is very defensive minded and a hard-working bunch is tough," Higgins recalls. "But that shows how the whole season was—never giving up and having confidence in our guys to go out and score two goals in two minutes or whatnot. Our line played a big role in it in that game, but if it wasn't our line doing it, it was Nicky's line or the defensemen. The biggest thing this year was just how deep our team was from top to bottom."

Parker doesn't recall the game quite as nostalgically. "That was pathetic. They just gave us that game. We gave it to them, and they gave it right back. It was unreal. Two teams that are going to be in the Hockey East final, and neither one of us could've sucked worse in the last eight minutes of that game."

In retrospect, perhaps the comeback win was not all that fortunate in the bigger picture. The victory gave the team its first No. 1 ranking in the USCHO poll all season, and they responded by going out to take a thumping from UMass, 5-1, much to the delight of over 7,000 fans at the Mullins Center in Amherst. The Minutemen's ostensible fourth line shut down the Wilson line and scored a goal to boot, so it was a humbling night for the Terriers. One small bright spot was Zach Cohen quietly scoring his first goal of the season.

Back at home on Sunday, BU rebounded with a 3-0 win over the crosstown Northeastern Huskies. Kieran Millan notched his first collegiate shutout, and Andrew Glass scored the first goal of his college career. "We just got outplayed," said Husky coach Greg Cronin afterwards. "I don't ever want to trade punches with a team like BU in terms of odd-man rushes, and that's what the first period was. I never thought we really got into a rhythm, and that has a lot to do with what BU did." Curiously, BU failed to score on many pretty plays, only to light the lamp on some gritty goals instead—much to Parker's delight.

It looked like the team was ready to go on a roll, and they did. Unfortunately, though, it would prove to be a downhill roll. The week to come would turn out to be the unequivocal low point of an otherwise terrific season.

There was no reason for apparent concern with

Vermont coming down to Boston for a Friday/Saturday doubleheader at Agganis. The bitterness of the season-ending loss to the Catamounts was now a more distant memory, given the shellacking the Terriers had put on their familiar foes up in Burlington just a few weeks back.

Friday's night game was a generally good effort for the home team, but Vermont showed real character in a game epitomized by their bend-but-don't-break mentality. BU took a 1-0 lead and outshot Vermont in every period— finishing with a 41-24 margin—but the scoreboard showed a see-saw battle. Vermont tied it at 1-1 and went ahead, only to have BU tie it. Vermont regained the lead in the third, only to have BU tie it 3-3 before Brayden Irwin redirected a shot from crafty playmaker Peter Lenes to give the visitors a 4-3 win.

In the post-game press conference, Parker called the game a "disguised effort" on the part of his squad. "They let us make some pretty plays and then they win the game. We had a lot of dipsy-doodle plays and looked like we were going to break it open any minute but didn't and gave them opportunities.

"I don't mind losing a game when my team plays real hard, when my team plays real smart. That was not the case tonight."

Parker's ire would only increase the following night. It was like the plot of *Groundhog Day* in some ways: BU takes lead, trades goals, ties the game 3-3 in the third, then loses 4-3. "To state the obvious, Vermont came in here and ate our lunch this weekend," Parker told the media. "They came in and got four points and dominated us in a bunch of different ways. They came in and dictated how the game had to be played on both nights, even more so tonight, I thought.

"We aren't patient enough to play the way you need to play against a team that doesn't want to come at you, that wants to play four or five men in center ice to clog up the middle."

73

MAD MEN

While BU's inability to adapt to Vermont's neutral-zone trap frustrated Parker, getting swept at home by the Catamounts absolutely incensed Matt Gilroy. Afterwards, the Terrier defenseman vented to assistant captain Brian Strait. "We were both really pissed off," Strait recalls. "We knew we were a lot better than that, and the effort that we gave and the carelessness… It just wasn't like us. I remember he stormed up to my room, fuming, right after the game on Saturday, and he said, 'I can't believe this. Coach is letting this happen: He didn't yell enough.'

"And I was saying, 'Calm down: It's the beginning of the season.' The next day we, the captains, went up to Coach and said, 'It's not going to happen again. We might lose another one—definitely we're not losing two in a row— but we're going to make sure that we're not going to play like that again.'

"And Coach was kind of the same way [as me]: 'Don't worry about it; it's the beginning of the season.' And we said, 'Look, we're just making sure you know that that's not going to happen again. It's unacceptable, and if anything like that ever happens again, you have all the right in the world to blow up at us.' But it didn't ever happen again. We lost a couple of games. Those were our third and fourth losses, that early in the season, and the whole rest of the season we only lost two more."

Yet the doldrums continued in the short term. Next up was a game against Atlantic Hockey rival Holy Cross. The coaches decided to bench Nick Bonino, who had cooled off dramatically after his torrid start. Taking away ice time by making a player a healthy scratch is often the m.o. to put the whole team on notice. After all, it's sometimes impossible to bench *every* player who may deserve to sit.

"That not only gets Bonino's attention, but it makes the rest of the boys say 'He benched Bonino? Well, I could be benched pretty quickly, too," Parker says. "Those types of things can help guys. It's happened to a whole bunch of

sophomores, forever. He got off to a great start. The puck
was jumping in the net for him. Then he stopped scoring
and started pressing, then he started thinking about
scoring goals. When you're playing hockey and you start
worrying about scoring goals, you *suck* at every other
aspect of the game, and then you never get the puck and
you never score the goal. He went the route that many
great players have gone."

Parker refuted the notion that scratching a highly
talented player is always his call; he told me that it could
be any of the coaching staff making the case. "One
of us would step up and say, 'What are we accepting
here?' This kid is supposed to be a ten-beller, and we're
accepting eight bells from him. Our staff has the ability
to say, 'Don't get fooled by this; don't accept mediocrity.'
Nick was not *trying* to be mediocre. He was just out
trying to do what he's supposed to do for our team but
going about it the wrong way, and he just didn't get it
until we had to sit him down and said, 'That's enough,
Nick.' Then he was pissed, but he realized, 'It must be
pretty bad if they're benching me.'"

Playing without Bonino, BU went out against the
Crusaders and emerged with their least inspiring victory
of the whole season, a 3-2 decision that was in doubt till
the final buzzer. After getting out to a 2-0 lead, the home
team just about called it a night. For the first time all
season, Parker reamed out his club between periods. "I
remember it probably took the first 10 or 12 games before
Coach came in the locker room and screamed at us to pick
it up," Jason Lawrence remembers. "Coach hadn't come
in and yelled us up to that point. So he yells at us, then he
walks out, walks back in, and says, 'I really haven't had to
yell at you guys for 12 games—that's amazing. I'm sorry
about this…"

Lawrence got called for slashing in the last minute,
giving Holy Cross a better chance to tie the game. The
senior would be benched for the subsequent game with

St. Lawrence as a result, but fingers could be pointed at any number of culprits, afterward. "In general, with the exception of a few guys, it was a pathetic performance by my team," Parker said at the press conference. "You've got to give Holy Cross credit for coming in and playing hard and saying 'Holy Jesus! This is BU? We can play with these guys… We can *more* than play with these guys.' And they did."

Escaping with a narrow win over an Atlantic Hockey opponent with a record around .500 and a ton of freshmen and sophomores in the lineup, Parker expressed more doubt about his team than at any time previously or subsequently during the season. "I think we fell into a trap of thinking we were better than we were and now we're in the trap of worrying about if we're as good as we ever were or as good as we can be," Parker said in the press conference. "We're so far away from where we were the first five or six game in terms of decision making and effort and skating. I thought Holy Cross looked quicker than we did.

"We're at the point where we're not sure if we're any good at all."

For his part, Matt Gilroy was mad as hell and not going to take it anymore. Taking matters into his own hands, Gilroy managed to earn the wrath of his coach at the next practice. "He refused to practice hard," Parker says. "It wasn't anything verbal he was doing. He was coasting through drills, and I made him do one again. So he did it even slower. There were some words said on the ice but most of it was his body language, and I finally said, 'Hey, screw.'"

Parker followed his co-captain into the locker room and gave him a tongue-lashing that harkened back to his earlier days of high-decibel coaching. "I got him out of his dressing room and into my dressing room, and I got in his face and said, 'Who the hell do you think you are?!' I thought this guy is too big for his britches."

However, it's revealing that Parker told me this story when I asked him to elaborate on something he said repeatedly later in the year—how Gilroy actually made him a better coach. "He's never ever admitted it, but I think he got himself thrown out of practice on purpose," Parker says. "I think what he was telling me was 'You should be doing this to everyone else; you're too easy on these guys right now.'" In light of Gilroy's complaint to Strait about Parker not getting mad enough with the team, it seems extremely likely that the altercation was a deliberate ploy on Gilroy's part.

Gilroy never mentioned the practice incident to me and instead credited his coach for the subsequent turnaround. "It wasn't talent; we just got outworked. And if you know Coach Parker, that's one thing he'll go crazy about. We got screamed at that week. 'How could you come here and let a team take two games from you in your own building? You're playing a team that prides itself on working hard. They say they know they can beat BU because they can outwork them. They come out and out-compete you: How can you just sit there and take it?' I know it woke up me and some of the older guys, and we said, 'We're not going to get outworked again.' And we realized that when we outwork teams, there's no team that can beat us."

SMOLDERING BOATS

The team bounced back with a satisfying 4-1 win against St. Lawrence over Thanksgiving weekend. Parker came into the press conference in high spirits, chuckling over his conversation with Saints' coach Joe Marsh, one of the funniest guys in college hockey. On a more serious note, though, Marsh described the game as "men against boys." It was a game that marked Bonino getting back in the lineup—centering McCarthy and Yip again—and it also showed signs of McCarthy realizing his offensive potential, picking up two assists.

"I definitely was not as confident offensively the first three years here as I was my senior year, when I got a little more ice time and little more opportunity offensively," he said. "It was a change of mindset on my part. The coaches were showing more faith in me by putting me in more offensive situations—putting me on the power play, putting me on a line with Nick and Brandon. That definitely changed things in my mind and gave me confidence from that faith the coaches put in me. I think I excelled this year because of it."

The trio would not be separated again all season. "All three of us just realized that we didn't want a roller coaster season," McCarthy says. "The two of them played great together before I was on the line, and I just did what I could to add to it. I went in the corners and did what I've always done here as far as playing defensively. Nick does a lot of things. He's a playmaker—he sees the ice well—but he also scores the goals. He's good down low defensively as far as being a center. Yipper's got a great shot, plays the point on the power play. He's also a goal scorer and a playmaker."

If the team needed any additional incentive to keep things rolling, a double date with archrival Boston College came along the very next weekend. By a wide margin, I can say that *all* of the most exciting "pre-January" college hockey games I have ever seen in my life have been BU-BC matchups. Much has been written about the rivalry over the years. Given the geographical proximity of the two programs—along with the fact that the most popular sport that they compete in is hockey—these are two teams that love to beat each other. Parker has often expressed how the standings and the stakes are not much of a factor in how motivational it is for the teams to face each other.

Back in 1985—my senior year at BU—the team had to play a game at Walter Brown Arena in front of no fans due to an outbreak of the measles. I often wonder what it would have been like to experience a BU-BC matchup in an empty arena like that, but I suspect that the level of intensity would be the same as usual.

With Grant Rollheiser nursing a groin injury at this point in the fall semester, the coaching staff had to abandon the netminding platoon for the first time of the season. Millan seized the reins and never really let them go the rest of the way. The front-end game at Agganis proved to be a goaltending spectacle, with Millan making 21 saves while BC's John Muse managed to stop 35 shots for a 1-1 deadlock. Any fans with weak bladders could have missed all of the scoring, which occurred in a 19-second span halfway through the first period.

That said, the low-scoring duel was by no means a snoozefest. "Great game to watch, great game to be involved in," Parker said. "Crowd was great, crowd was into it. In reality it should've been 5-5 instead of 1-1. There were so many great chances; it wasn't like there was nothing happening out there. Goalies played great. Guys had great opportunities and missed nets."

BC had to be pleased to obtain a tie on the road despite getting outshot dramatically. Conditions looked favorable for the Eagles to pull out three of four points with a Saturday night win at Conte Forum. Instead, the Terriers upped the ante and earned the right to enjoy the short trip home following a 3-1 victory.

Freshman Chris Connolly got the game-winning goal on a penalty shot of all things, and USCHO's Jim Connolly reported that Parker called a key timeout with BC pressing midway through the third. BU got called for an icing, and a recently adopted rule is that a team can't change on-ice personnel immediately after icing the puck. The timeout gave the team a breather, and the BU defense clamped down on the Eagles for the next several minutes. BC threatened several times with the goalie pulled until Bonino potted an empty-net goal from long distance with one second left.

Another matchup with the River Hawks was the only

game remaining before Christmas Break. That game provided additional proof of the Terriers' depth. Often, a team's fourth line is an energy line—skating hard, making some hits, playing good D. This year, the Terriers had three fourth-liners who amassed respectable point totals despite limited ice time. In this game, Popko, Pereira, and Zach Cohen not only ratcheted up the energy; they also buried BU's first two goals of the game. Pereira, the self-proclaimed "Bulldog", scored the first goal off a rebound and later took a quick-release shot that Cohen tucked in.

It was what Parker called a "tooth and nail" game, as it was tied 2-2 through two periods despite BU enjoying a 21-9 edge in attempted shots during that second stanza. Strangely, though, Lowell lost another starting goalie to injury in the second period—just as had occurred a month ago. Finally, Colin Wilson set up Colby Cohen for a one-timer from the left-wing side. The shot caromed off of Chris Higgins's skate and into the net to make it a 3-2 final—but only after Lowell hit a pipe with the goalie pulled.

Many of the first-semester wins had not been easy. In some, the margins looked lopsided, deceptively. Quite a few others were in doubt up until the last minute. Gradually, though, it seemed like the team was developing an identity. Win big or win a squeaker, but make sure you win.

It was not clear whether they had fully internalized the mentality of burning the boats—yet they definitely showed signs of smoldering.

FINAL SCORE AT END OF PERIOD ONE:

Boston University Record: 11 Wins, 4 Losses, 1 Tie
Goals: Boston University 57, Opponents 34
Championships: Ice Breaker

SECOND PERIOD

Regular Season: Spring Semester

ROCKY MOUNTAIN HEIST

The next opportunity to obtain hardware arrived in early January with the Denver Cup, and a pair of victories would ensure a decidedly happier new year. It would be a challenge, however. While first-round opponent Rensselaer had struggled thus far, beating Denver at high altitude in their home rink—a venue that Jack Parker has described as similar to a Southwestern mission complete with bell tower—would be no easy feat.

To add another degree of difficulty, the Terriers would be without two of their better players. Colin Wilson and Kevin Shattenkirk had been selected to represent the United States at the World Junior Championships for Under-20 players. While they competed in Ottawa, others would have to step up to fill their skates.

Like Zach Cohen earlier in the season, Steve Smolinsky had become an almost forgotten player after surviving the near purge back in the spring. With freshman defenseman Ryan Ruikka sidelined indefinitely due to a shoulder injury, Smolinsky was next in line to play defense if necessary. But with six defensemen ahead of him on the depth chart—all of them NHL prospects—he was not about to supplant anyone based on skill.

No one had been injured to date—and Smolinsky told me emphatically that he never wanted to get into the lineup that way—so he had played exactly one of the first 16 games of the season, filling in when the coaches made Colby Cohen a healthy scratch against St. Lawrence. That had been a blunt reminder to Cohen that he needed to play both ends of the ice instead of focusing mostly on offense. Meanwhile, freshman Chris Connolly received the nod to fill in for Wilson on the first line.

The result in the opening game turned out to be a misleading 6-2 final against Rensselaer. On the negative side of the ledger, the Terriers looked a little flat after the holiday layoff. They gave up a shorthanded goal midway through the second period, and it was a 2-2 game late in the second before a pair of Jason Lawrence goals broke it open late in the second and the third.

More positively, Zach Cohen, Kevin Gilroy, and Luke Popko scored goals with the team missing some of its stars. The last two goals of the night—scored by Popko and Yip—occurred in a span of just 30 seconds. That was the fourth time that feat had been accomplished, so by now that phenomenon had quietly become a recurring theme.

Speaking of which, both of Lawrence's goals came on the power play, and the senior winger was on his way to becoming one of the nation's top scorers with the man advantage. He would end up tied for third in the country with 25 goals while finishing second nationally with 14 power-play goals.

Amusingly, Lawrence also became the equivalent to a football running back who scores tons of touchdowns on plunges from the one-yard line. He must have had at least 15 goals that he scored from within five feet of the net over the course of the year. "They would joke that

that's my office—right around the goal," Lawrence says. "That's where I play. I'm not a guy that's going to take it end to end, beat four guys, and then roof it from the top of the circle. I just hang around the net and find some loose pucks, try to make some passes."

If the first night in Denver looked shaky early for the visiting Terriers, the championship game proved to be quite another matter. In a matchup of teams ranked in the top five nationally, No. 3 BU raced out of the gate, outshooting No. 5 Denver 13-2 in the early going and taking a 2-0 lead on goals by Vinny Saponari and Matt Gilroy.

Denver made it interesting with a Rhett Rakhshani goal late in the second period, but Bonino made a nice play on a faceoff to set up Yip to get that one back 74 seconds later. Up 3-1, BU went into a defensive shell in the third period, surrendering a bunch of shots but no goals. The score remained unchanged until Zach Cohen notched an empy-net goal in the waning seconds for a 4-1 final. Soon co-captains McCarthy and Gilroy were hoisting the team's second trophy of the year, the Wells Fargo Denver Cup.

"It was going to be a test," Yip recalls. "We didn't have Willie and Shatty, and they had played a big role on our team up till that point. Willie had been on fire, and Shatty had put up great numbers while playing great defensively. Still, we had guys that we knew could fill in with them out. Smolinsky jumped in and did an unbelievable job; he was one of our best d-men that weekend. He was rushing the puck; he was hitting— doing everything. It was like he was never out of the lineup."

It certainly didn't feel that way to Smolinsky. "It was extremely nerve-wracking," he says. "With defense, everyone notices your mistakes more." Smolinsky didn't make many mistakes that weekend. In fact, Bernie Corbett recalled one writer that weekend gushing with praise about #8, not knowing he was the team's seventh defenseman. The writer made a lofty comparison to NHL defenseman Brian Rafalski, a smallish but offensively gifted defenseman with excellent skating ability.

Afterwards, Corbett overheard Denver coach George Gwozdecky raving about the Terriers to the local media. "That team has everything. They have a great core of leadership. They have skill. They're fast. A team hasn't played us like that all year." Considering that the team had played without two of its top players, Corbett believed that the compliment boded well.

ROCKING TOWARD A MILESTONE

With Wilson and Shattenkirk back on hand, BU overcame a sluggish start, playing great in the third period as it rolled over Maine back home on January 10, winning 4-1 behind two goals from Chris Connolly, who had settled back onto the third line. One year earlier, they were 5-10-3 on this date. Now they were 14-4-1 and first in the PairWise Rankings, the mathematical system devised to determine how teams are seeded in the national tournament after the regular season and postseason are completed.

The next game resulted in a surprising loss to Providence. After a fall semester in which they had received abysmal goaltending, the Friars brought in a January freshman named Alex Beaudry. The Terriers peppered him with 41 shots while giving up just 21, but Beaudry made 39 saves while Grant Rollheiser stopped just 16 of 20 shots. Several were due to what Parker described as "unbelievable mistakes" by the skaters, yet it was after this game that the coaching staff finally abandoned the rotation and went with Millan as the number-one goalie for the rest of the season.

It wasn't as if anyone ever stopped believing that Rollheiser ultimately would turn out to be a really good goalie. Millan simply had been the better player, and goaltending coach Mike Geragosian felt that Rollheiser had some holes in his game at that time. Meanwhile, Millan had fully earned the trust of his teammates. "I know he's just a freshman, but the kid just doesn't let goals in," Colby Cohen says. "He was great every time he put his stuff on. As a defenseman, you never had to go out and say, 'Are you okay?' In practice, we joke around all the time, but as far as a game goes not once did I have to skate out to the net and say do this or do that. You've just got to let him do his thing, and you'll get the best product."

BU won a truly ugly game up at Merrimack three days later, with the teams combining for a whopping 97 penalty minutes. The game got out of hand in the third period, and Parker was enraged when Higgins and Matt Gilroy were hit into the boards from behind without any major penalties being called. Higgins suffered a concussion and could not play the next night. It also looked bad for Gilroy, who received a dislocated shoulder.

If the official word was that Gilroy might be out for awhile, co-captain McCarthy indicated that Gilroy getting back in the lineup the next night was no surprise whatsoever. "Not at all. Something that everyone on this team realizes is that Matt wants to play and wants to win, and he's going to do everything he can to do that. So if there's any chance that he can play, he will. It wasn't as if he was going to injure himself any more than he already was; it was just going to hurt. Everyone knew he was going to play, and he did."

"When I got the word Saturday afternoon that he was going to play, it was just a huge sigh of relief," Bernie Corbett remembers. "The only thing I can equate it to is what happened in '95. Down the stretch, things were falling into place for the team, and Steve Thornton hurt his knee. He's our first-line center; it looks like he's going to be out for a while, and he played in the next game."

Of course, the recuperative powers of almost any Terrier were going to be at their highest when the next opponent was BC—especially when a win or tie would make BU the winners of the regular-season series, always a feather in the helmet for either program.

When it came time to drop the puck, BC scored 40 seconds into the game, but it was all downhill from there for the Eagles. They would not score again until the game's last 70 seconds. Meanwhile, BU scored five unanswered goals, including four on the power play. With the shots ending up 46-21 in favor of the Terriers, it could have been even more lopsided than the 5-2 final if not for an excellent effort by Eagle goalie John Muse in net.

In addition to the subplot of Gilroy getting back in the lineup, another bit of intrigue arose around Colby Cohen. For the second time in the season, Cohen had been a healthy scratch the night before against Merrimack. How would he respond to the benching? As it turns out, he went from the doghouse to top dog with the game-winning goal and an assist, earning recognition from the media as the No. 1 star of the game.

"First time I was kind of annoyed," Cohen recalls about the two healthy scratches. "I had played a lot of good games and then played one bad game and was getting sat. Getting sat is tough, and Coach Parker is tough on me because he wants to get the best out of me. You never want to admit it, but you've got to say that there's a method to his madness."

The win against BC set the stage for what arguably could be called BU's best performance in a regular-season game all year, a resounding 5-0 whitewashing of UNH at Agganis Arena. It was the first line's night to shine, with Wilson, Higgins, and Lawrence combining for three goals and six assists. It was especially encouraging to see Higgins return from his concussion to notch three helpers on the night, but the true star was the team's Predator-to-be. "Colin Wilson played great tonight," Parker said at the press conference. "He was the best player on the ice both offensively and defensively."

Parker then laughed a little ruefully, mindful of the sophomore's looming pro career. "I don't think we'll have him after this semester so we might wear him out." Meanwhile, Millan ran his record to an eyebrow-raising 13-1-1 with the shutout.

The next night, the teams completed the home-and-home series up at the Whittemore Center. As a program, UNH has not had a losing record since the 1995-96 season—easily the longest stretch of any Hockey East team. In fact, I believe that Michigan is the only program that has a longer streak, unless you include Colorado College, which has had a couple of years right at or just above .500 in that timeframe.

The Whit is a great venue for watching hockey. Even though it is a difficult place for most visitors to play, BU has had more success there of any Wildcat opponent. In fact, they are the only team to hold a winning record on UNH's home ice. This game proved that rule, as the team pulled out a 3-1 win. The Terriers now have a 9-6-5 record at the Whit.

As Melissa Parrelli reported afterward for USCHO, Parker raved yet again about the play of Millan. "All in all that game was won in two aspects; number one was our goaltending, he played absolutely wonderful. And [number two] we did a good job killing penalties tonight. And when we didn't, when [the Wildcats] got great looks because they moved it so well and we were out of position, Kieran once again came up big for us. Those are the two reasons we're walking out of here with two points."

"Beanpot Season" loomed in the near distance, but the media knows better than to ask Parker anything about it until after the previous Friday's game. In this case, Matt Gilroy notched a goal and an assist in less than two minutes during the first period as two steps toward a 3-1 win at Merrimack, giving Parker his 800th coaching victory. As he always does, Parker was quick to credit the milestone to his many assistant coaches and recruiters over the years.

BEAN COUNTERS

With that win under his belt, Parker and the City of Boston prepared for the 57th Beanpot tournament. Played at the TD Banknorth Garden, home of the Boston Bruins, the mystique of the Beanpot is perhaps difficult for outsiders to appreciate. It is basically the college hockey championship for the four teams in the immediate Boston area: BU, BC, Northeastern, and Harvard.

Between the venue with its enormous crowd and its unusual timing on the first two Mondays of February, it is a major event. For any team that wins it in a given year, it is a quick way to lay claim to a successful season—regardless of your final record. In fact, Parker has mentioned that some casual fans seem to believe that the season *ends* with the Beanpot championship and that winning it is the *only* measure of a local team's success.

Historically, the Terriers have dominated the tournament, winning exactly half of the first 56 tournaments going into this year's classic. BC had won exactly one-fourth of the titles—14 total—while Harvard had won it ten times. Northeastern had only won all the beans four times. BU and BC had been exclusive champions going back to Harvard's win in 1993, while NU had not won since 1988—just over a month after Brian Strait was born.

Of course, all of that was ancient history. While some scribes have dubbed the tournament the BU Invitational, every February offers the possibility of a change to the status quo. For the 2009 Beanpot, the college hockey cognoscenti generally proclaimed that three of the four teams had a good chance to take home the pot of gold. Despite Northeastern's long drought in early February, coach Greg Cronin had led the team beyond respectability and into a first-place position in Hockey East going into February. As defending national champions, BC had experienced a bit of roller coaster season, but they obviously had the talent and experience to win another Beanpot.

To date, BU owned a 19-5-1 record and appeared to have the most talent of the four teams. Then there was Harvard, slogging along with a 5-11-4 record. It made sense that the BC-NU semifinal game would be a cliffhanger that could go either way, while BU would win a rout over Harvard.

As it turned out, the opposite occurred. Northeastern beat BC decisively, while the Terriers and Crimson battled it out in a game that wasn't absolutely decided until *after* the final buzzer.

What made the game so close? One factor was that Terrier goalie Kieran Millan, ordinarily a pillar of placidity, went into the game feeling nervous for the first time all season. "Everyone talked about the Beanpot, and I'd never heard about it growing up. I never watched college hockey, so I didn't understand it. There was just so much hype. I just felt that if we lose, it's all my fault. But having that nervous game against Harvard helped me play better in the Beanpot final and in the Hockey East semifinal and final."

"I thought Harvard played unbelievably hard throughout the game," Parker said afterwards. "We were getting outworked in the first period ... We played better in second period, and I thought maybe we'd have momentum in the third period. But then I thought Harvard played their best in the third."

Millan looked jumpy, and Harvard stunned the favorites by going out to a 2-0 lead early in the second period. Michael Biega's opening goal—an innocuous-looking wrist shot that eluded Millan's right leg en route to the far corner—provided the first indication that the Terrier goalie might not be at his best.

The second goal came on a two-man advantage, but Millan looked unhappy with himself when Alex Killorn's wrister found a good-sized gap on the short side. BU failed to get on the board until after the midway point in the game, when Bonino came up big with two goals in under two minutes to tie it up.

"When I'm involved in a goal or when I score, there's a confidence that comes with that," Bonino says, attempting to explain his knack for scoring in bunches. "I know when I scored the first one against Harvard, I just remember thinking 'everything feels right.' You get the puck again, and you're more comfortable with it and able to make that second goal. When you're not scoring, you just get down and down on yourself."

Months later, Mike Bavis marvels at Gilroy's assist on the equalizer. "On the power play, the puck was dumped in. Gilroy raced down on the wall, and as soon as he got it, he just took it right out of the corner and started to attack the net. He just threw a little saucer pass over to Bonino, who pulled it around the goalie. He beat the guy right off the wall. It's a very unusual play for that kind of opening to take place."

Gilroy would make another great move culminating in a backhanded pass to Bonino again in Washington, D.C., so in retrospect it's hard to look at that highlight without thinking of greater stakes to come.

At that point, it looked like Harvard would fold like a tent in a hurricane of Terrier offense. That never happened. At 9:00 of the third period, Michael Biega raced in on the left wing and clanged one off a post for the Crimson before BU finally took its first lead of the night. Zach Cohen scored the biggest goal of his career—up to that point—when an offensive-end draw won by Luke Popko led to Cohen's bad-angle shot from the very bottom of the left-wing face-off circle, banking it off of Harvard goalie Matt Hoyle's arm and into the net.

Still, it was far from over. Millan gave up perhaps his

most excruciating goal of the year with just over five minutes left. Alex Biega took a shot from the point, and the puck went through a crowd before bouncing off Millan and bleeding across the goal line for a 3-3 tie.

BU picked up a power play late in the game, and Jason Lawrence got the puck with 1:46 left. Instead of one of his characteristic tap-ins at the far post, Lawrence wound up and blasted a powerful slapshot from the left-wing circle, beating Hoyle up high on the glove side. "It was a little uncharacteristic," Lawrence told me afterwards, outside the dressing room. "My dad always yells at me to take the high slapshot. Luckily I listened to him for once and put my head down, and it went in, so that was good."

You can always count on hockey players for understatement.

Remarkable for such a blast, Lawrence was actually aiming his shot. "I was sort of cheating a little bit. I was thinking glove side," he said.

Still, there was further drama to come. As the final seconds ticked down, Harvard desperately pressured the Terrier net. As time expired, it was the dangerous defenseman Alex Biega shooting the puck into the net, and the Crimson celebrated as the referee signaled that it was a goal.

The only problem for Harvard was that the puck was nowhere near crossing the goal line when the final buzzer sounded. A video review took a good while, but Parker was unconcerned. "I knew it was no goal," Parker said. "I couldn't see what was happening in the corner, so I was watching on the Jumbotron. It was 0:00 before anybody started screaming, so I knew when they went upstairs that it would be no goal."

Parker didn't have to go very far back into his considerable memory banks to find a comparable sporting event. "The first thing I could think of as the game unwound and the buzzer went off was that this was like the Super Bowl yesterday," Parker said, alluding to the

Pittsburgh Steelers nail-biting victory over the Arizona Cardinals. "Who's going to get the last shot? Who's going to get the last chance?"

It definitely was BU's first dodged bullet in a high-stakes game. It would not be the last.

Another idiosyncrasy of the Beanpot is that it's the only tournament I can think of in which the teams play a non-tournament game between the semifinal and final. I like to call it the "Beanpot Intermission" game. Parker always frets about his team being distracted on that Friday night, but the fact of the matter is that BU is 21-2-1 over the past 24 times playing the game between those first two fateful Mondays in February.

Goalie coach Mike Geragosian wasn't thinking about that record at all in preparation for the Friday game against Lowell. Instead, his focus would be on ensuring that his young netminder regained his confidence after his first real struggle of the season at the Garden. "Psychologically, we brought him back after the Beanpot," Geragosian says. "I told Jack, 'You can't just bring things back for a 19-year-old kid the next day. It takes a week— sometimes two weeks. Like in baseball, think of Big Papi's slump' [in the first few months of the 2009 Red Sox season, slugger David Ortiz struggled mightily].

"What happened was I talked to Kieran about sunshine, let it go, positive imagery. It's very important, the psychology of this. I talk a lot to [BU sports psychologists] Leonard Zaichkowsky, Adam Naylor, and Cindy Adams about how to handle goaltenders. We talk a lot about resilience."

Geragosian didn't stop there. He pulled together his somewhat offense-happy defensive corps to make sure they would provide more support than usual in their own end on Friday night. "I told the defense for the Lowell game, 'Listen, let's *really* play tight D. Let's not jump up in the play, and let's get some confidence going—have him make a few stops.'

"If you watch that Lowell game, the first three or four shots he looked real jumpy, but the defense cleared them. Then all of a sudden when he got a period under his belt, he was fine. So that situation was settled with positive imagery: You're going to see sunshine, you're going to bounce back, let it go, you'll be fine, we believe in you."

With Millan's psyche repaired successfully, the team continued its positive run in the Beanpot Intermission game, topping Lowell 5-3. It was an odd game, though, as Parker's worries about the team lacking focus looked anything from paranoid to plausible over the course of the evening. Early on, it was like an old-time Chicago political election, as BU scored early and often. David Warsofsky and Joe Pereira scored 59 seconds apart in the first period, and then John McCarthy potted another 52 seconds after that. With those three goals, the tally for two goals in less than a minute had now reached six for the season.

Then the Terriers turned around and blew that 3-0 lead before pulling out a win in the last ten minutes of the game.

After amassing just two points all season, Eric Gryba notched two assists in under two minutes. Afterward, the junior had a hard time recalling his last multi-point game. "It hasn't been here," Gryba said, amused at his rare appearance at a press conference. "It wasn't in junior hockey. Probably in midget hockey. I'm rarely down [near the opposing net], and I was surprised to find myself down there, to tell you the truth."

Along with Brian Strait, Gryba undoubtedly was a true unsung hero of this year's team. By this point in the season, it was obvious that Gryba had made great strides as a player. Always a physical presence, Gryba had sometimes made bad decisions as a freshman and sophomore—including taking some dumb penalties. This year he was unbelievably consistent and a bedrock in his own end.

93

"With Strait and Gryba, we don't have a lot of what they give us," associate head coach and former Terrier defenseman David Quinn says, alluding to the fact that the team's other four defensemen are more inclined to think of offense first. "Those two guys were indispensable. Gryba to me really made the biggest jump of any of them. His skating improved dramatically. People forget he's 20 years old. He grew up. If you look at the D corps, a lot of them are going to play in the NHL, but he might have the longest career of any of them. He doesn't need anyone else [to be valuable to a team]. He needs to defend, play hard, be physical, and make an outlet pass. What's very underrated about him are his puck skills. He can pass the puck and sees the ice well."

So after that sigh of relief, all eyes would be riveted on the BU-NU Beanpot championship. Over on Huntington Avenue, Husky fans made a good deal of noise about how this could be the year for the Huskies to end their bean famine at last. It made sense. Goalie Brad Thiessen was well on his way to earn Hockey East Player of the Year honors as well as being named as one of the Hobey Baker Hat Trick finalists. Meanwhile, Millan was just a freshman, and he had looked a little shaky during his first appearance on the big stage. On top of that, BU kept winning games but couldn't seem to oust NU from the top spot in the league standings.

All of the talk about the possibility of an overdue Husky championship eventually grated on the Terrier players. "Going into the game, that whole Northeastern thing of 'Oh, we haven't won it in a long time and we're the better team'—that really motivated everybody," Colin Wilson says. "We're tired of hearing that."

It turned out to be yet another nailbiter with a deceptively lopsided score. Colby Cohen pinged a shot off a post and in to make it 1-0 in the first period, only to have Husky forward Mike McLaughlin rifle one under the crossbar with less than 30 seconds remaining in the period to tie it.

Often a goal in a period's last minute ignites a team, and an ensuing Husky power play might have led Northeastern to believe they could get a goal in the second period's first minute as well. Instead, Brandon Yip stole the puck and skated in shorthanded. His shot missed the net but caromed off the boards, and Bonino buried the rebound to make it 2-1, BU.

Northeastern tied the game again 10:01, but BU regained the lead just 65 seconds later on a Jason Lawrence goal. After his atypical slapshot against Harvard, Lawrence returned to his usual specialty for this one, as Chris Higgins fired a great pass from the left-wing wall for Lawrence to tap in at the far post. For the moment, it started to appear that BU would answer whenever necessary.

However, you could sense the momentum swinging gradually but significantly toward Northeastern as the third period wore on. Sometimes intuition tells you when a goal is coming, and the Husky fans were rowdy and excited as the final frame wore on. Fortunately for BU, Millan absolutely proved to be on his game that night, especially during a two-man advantage for the Huskies early in the third period.

Still, the stage appeared to be set for an NU equalizer with 7:06 remaining. Northeastern had just killed a penalty successfully, and then Joe Pereira was sent off for a foolish slashing penalty. The Huskies had a power play and a fantastic opportunity to tie it up. Instead, the shorthanded Terriers delivered a one-two punch that sent their opponent to the canvas.

At 6:06, on a shorthanded two-on-one, David Warsofsky shot the puck off the post and in on Thiessen's glove side. Then—all of 30 seconds later—Kevin Shattenkirk and Colin Wilson found themselves on *another* shorthanded two-on-one, with Wilson finishing it off after a great dish from the sophomore defensemen.

For the seventh time of the season, it was a burst of two goals in under a minute. Shaking their heads over two Terrier defensemen leading shorthanded rushes for the goals, the Husky fans quietly filed out in a mass exodus. In this case, a total of three shorthanded goals equaled game, set, and match for the Terriers. "I've never seen that in my life in the Beanpot," Parker said. "Special teams were big for us, just in a different way than I thought it would be."

"It all happened so fast that I think we were shocked," Cronin said.

MAJORING IN UNFINISHED BUSINESS

The Terriers reveled in winning Boston's big prize on top of nailing down the third of three possible tournament championships. The players joyfully carried the weighty trophy around the Garden ice, passing it from captains to seniors to juniors and so forth, as is the tradition. Remarkably, BU had now won more than half of the titles in Beanpot history. But as John McCarthy remembers, the excitement was trumped by a greater sense of unfinished business. He believes that the ensuing days marked one of Parker's best motivational moves of the year. "After the Beanpot, there was a celebration that night, and everyone was happy. But when we got back to practice, he made it clear that we're sick of just winning Beanpots: We want to win something bigger. We have more to win.

"He made sure that we had a hard week of practice the next week because we had to get ready for the playoffs, and we needed to boost our national ranking for the NCAAs. I thought he was good at that this year. He let us enjoy our wins, enjoy our success, but there was always this sense that we had more to win, and I think everyone on the team bought into that: We're not done yet; this isn't good enough. We want more."

Playing the first of a pair of games after the long drive up to Orono, Maine, that weekend, BU certainly showed no signs of a Beanpot hangover—unlike the 1995 championship team, which received an old-fashioned whupping at Providence in its first game after winning the Beanpot.

On Friday, the first line had one of its best games of the season. Just 16 seconds into the game, Colin Wilson scored on a wrister under the crossbar, and the rout was on. Starting Black Bear goalie Scott Darling yielded four goals on BU's first six shots before getting yanked early in the second period. By then, the game was basically over. Wilson ended up with a hat trick with the third goal coming on a perfect cross-ice pass from Matt Gilroy. Jason Lawrence added two goals, and Wilson, Lawrence, Higgins combined for a whopping ten points between them.

Saturday night was another story. After being outshot by Maine on Friday despite the lopsided score in its favor, BU enjoyed a huge advantage in terms of shot totals but fell behind 2-0 and had to fight back to pick up a 2-2 tie. Nick Bonino's second effort with a rebound shot off of a faceoff finally brought the Terriers even with less than five minutes to play in regulation. Altogether, it seemed like a case of the Terriers taking the Black Bears for granted after having their way with them in the opener.

When they returned from Orono, the players noticed another addition to the spectacular locker room. Above each player's locker, there was now a three-foot by one-foot placard featuring color photos of each player along with his name, number, and hometown. It was easy to picture a teenaged recruit coming in and imagining himself among the ranks of the Terriers.

The new trimmings would not make an iota of difference against Northeastern that weekend, however. Despite the fact that the Terriers had claimed the top spot in the PairWise Rankings in the national picture, they were still trying to oust the Huskies from first place in the Hockey East standings. Northeastern got off to an impressive 13-3-1 start in league play through late January, leaving the rest of the league in the rearview mirror for much of the season. Now a home-and-home series would give the Terriers an opportunity catch the frontrunners at last.

The atmosphere in both arenas was phenomenal that weekend, as Eric Gryba recalls. "Our crowd was unbelievable the first night—one of the best crowds we had all year—and their crowd the next night was electric. You couldn't hear yourself think out there."

BU appeared poised to capitalize in the standings in the first period at Agganis on Friday night, racing out to a 2-0 lead. Then the home team frittered away the lead, as NU responded with two second-period goals. The third period was a defensive-minded chess match for the most part; it felt like playoff hockey. In the end, it was a 2-2 final and a missed opportunity for BU in particular, given that it was a home game. It might have even been a better result than BU deserved that night. Millan needed to make a game-saving stop on Tyler McNeely in the last minute of overtime in order for BU to hang on.

"We played a pretty good first period and then we acted like the game was over, up 2-0," Parker told USCHO writer Dave Hendrickson afterward. "The difference between Northeastern's effort, determination, awareness and positional play compared to ours was like night and day... We were unbelievably fortunate to get a point. We really dodged a bullet. That team outplayed us for the last 40 minutes. It was a great show by them and a sad show by us."

More bad news emerged on Friday. In the second period, Chris Higgins received a hit from behind, and his hand got jammed into the boards. "Going into the third period, my hand was throbbing," Higgins recalls. "I could barely hold my stick, and I knew something was wrong. That was on a Friday night, and on Saturday morning I couldn't hold my stick. Our trainer Larry

Venis tried to work on the soft tissue, but I still couldn't get a grip. I went out for warm-ups but just couldn't play that night. It was tough not being able to play that night. I can't imagine what it was like for fans watching the Miami game; I was having a heart attack just watching Northeastern."

Reduced to observer status for the back end of the weekend series, Higgins would fail to be his old self again until receiving a cortisone shot shortly before the NCAA tournament. Unsurprisingly, his production down the stretch would suffer—particularly in the Hockey East tournament.

Meanwhile, the Huskies and Terriers staged a classic dogfight at Matthews Arena on Saturday evening. Matthews is one of the rowdiest arenas in the league. The student section, known as the Doghouse, has fans sitting—or standing, more accurately—in the upper tier of the old arena. The Doghouse is behind and above the goal that Northeastern attacks in the first and third periods, so the boisterous fans are almost right on top of the opposing goaltender. Naturally, they never let him forget that they are looming over him. It makes for quite a scene.

In this game, it was a night of great goaltending to match the intense atmosphere, as both teams failed to score through the first 47 minutes. Finally, in an echo of BU's Beanpot win, the Terriers took the third-period lead, as a shorthanded two-on-one bedeviled the Huskies once again. Bonino raced in and made a great cross to Matt Gilroy, who beat Brad Thiessen at the far-side post. Unlike the Beanpot, though, Northeastern managed to tie it up with just 2:22 left in regulation when Joe Vitale passed to Steve Quailer on the doorstep.

The Terriers hung in late, killing one penalty at the end of regulation and another when Brandon Yip—an increasing fixture in the penalty box—was called for a five-minute major with just over a minute left in overtime. The final was a hard-earned 1-1 tie that left both coaches catching their breath.

"What do you say about that game?" Northeastern coach Greg Cronin told Keith Lavon of USCHO after the game. "It was an incredibly emotional game. If you were going to say Northeastern was going to have ten power-plays and BU was going to have nine, and neither one of them would score, I would say it would be the most bizarre game you would ever see."

Despite the same outcome as the night before, Parker was happier with his team's performance. "I'd say these teams are real close; I didn't think last night's game was anywhere near as exciting, anywhere near as well played as this game."

PET PEEVES

The two teams would stay real close right up to the end of the regular season. Still, the immediate upshot of the weekend was that BU came out of it the same way they went in—one point behind the frontrunners in the standings. While this was somewhat disappointing, Parker was far more troubled by something else he had sensed around that time. The team's psyche had gradually taken a negative turn, and team spirit appeared to be on thin ice. None of this was mentioned to the media at the time, but the following week proved to be a turning point for the season and Parker's best moment as a coach during the championship year.

As Jason Lawrence says, Parker is excellent at focusing on the tactical elements early in the season. "People like to focus on the games, but I think it's what he does in practice to break the game down—the power play or the forecheck. He makes it so easy to understand—on a daily basis you learn something new." However, as the schedule intensifies in January, February, and March, Lawrence indicates that Parker's focus changes. "Then you kind of feed off of his competitiveness. It translates into how you try to beat guys in practice. X's and O's take care of themselves—you learn those in the first month and a half—after that it's the will to win."

After the Northeastern series, Parker believed that the team had lost its focus on that will to win. Any Bill Russell video on being a great teammate or stirring speech from a Jack O'Callahan or Mike Grier now looked distant in the rearview mirror. The team now seemed distracted by any number of other issues. In particular, the players had been bickering about which player was the pet of the various coaches. In typical fashion, Parker attacked the problem head-on.

"There was a team meeting after the Northeastern doubleheader ties," Parker remembers. "There were a lot of problems going on with the team, and we had gotten away from being BU hockey players, I thought. Too many guys were worried about bullshit again, so we decided to air the laundry. I was the one who started about what was perceived to be going on. Everybody perceived that the coaches were kissing certain guys' asses. 'They don't like me, but they like him.'"

Parker set the players straight. "In reality, you guys have no idea what conversations take place away from the ice," he told them. "It's a completely different situation than most of you think it is, but you've got to get over this bullshit. Now all it is, is, 'I wonder if I'm going to be on the All-Hockey East team?' If *that* shit is creeping in, we've got problems. So there's my problem: You're all getting selfish again. So-and-so is Bavo's pet, and so-and-so is Quinny's boy and Parker thinks that everybody sucks except Higgins. So grow the fuck up."

After Parker gave the players that blunt piece of his mind, he gave everyone else a chance to make any comments or air any grievances. "So everybody got involved and talked about it, and the fact that we got everybody involved was real good," Parker says. "I'll never forget it: The best practice we had was when we went right from that meeting to practice that day. They all had fun; they all were going hard as hell, and it was like 'Whoa, we're a team again.'"

"It happens in every locker room; it happens with every team," David Quinn says. "That had to be brought to the forefront, and Jack attacked it head on. We don't have any 'guys'; we love you all. And we're not going anywhere unless we're all pulling in the same direction. At that point, we had only lost one game since late November. But you could sense it; you could feel it in practice. And right then and there, it was a like a cloud had been lifted off of everybody's shoulders."

Parker didn't stop there. He had some meetings with small groups of players. Kevin Shattenkirk recalls being pulled in with classmates Colby Cohen and Colin Wilson. Parker reminded his young stars that they were supposed to be a focal point of the team but that they had been falling short on the ice. "It really lit a fire under us," Shattenkirk says.

MASS PRODUCTION

In retrospect, it seems likely that the team's refreshed psyche factored into the improbable result at Amherst on the following Friday night. You often hear about how awful it is for a hockey team to give up a goal in the first or last minute of a period. Already trailing 1-0 to UMass in front of a boisterous road crowd of 8,291 fans, BU gave up another goal with 56 seconds left in the first period. Fifty-five seconds after the first intermission, the Terriers surrendered another tally to make it a 3-0 deficit.

Over the radio, I could hear the Minuteman fans chanting "Overrated," which seemed premature for a game that was only 21 minutes old. Still, for the first time all season, Parker resorted to pulling Kieran Millan early in a game in an attempt to jumpstart his team.

Within three minutes of that decision, Matt Gilroy scored to make it 3-1. Nick Bonino picked up an assist on that goal, and the team had not lost all season when the sophomore scored at least one point. "I started hearing it toward the last third of the season," Bonino says. "I remember we were down 3-0 to UMass and I got an assist when we made it 3-1, and I remember thinking almost subconsciously, 'Every time I've got a point we've won. Is it going to end tonight?'"

Sure enough, Gilroy scored again eight minutes later to pull the Terriers within a goal. Then, remarkably, Jason Lawrence notched a natural hat trick within a span of less than seven minutes. Meanwhile, Grant Rollheiser looked great in relief of Millan, stopping all ten shots he faced. All in all, BU steamrollered UMass with six unanswered goals and came away with a 6-3 win.

Back at Agganis for the tail end of the home-and-home against UMass, it was more of the same... and then some. After yielding just the first goal, the Terriers one-upped the previous night's performance by scoring *seven* unanswered goals en route to a 7-2 win.

Almost predictably, though, Parker's perspective on the weekend was not necessarily what a more casual observer would have expected. As always with Parker, he is generally the opposite of the fan who responds to any critique of his team by pointing at the scoreboard. His satisfaction—or lack thereof—revolves around whether the team is playing well and *deserving* of a good outcome, regardless of the actual score.

"I thought we were horrible in the first period," Parker said immediately after Saturday's romp. "I thought they were good, and we were real bad—not taking care of the puck, not skating. Last night after being down 2-0, I went into the dressing room and said, 'You're playing well— just keep playing hard. I like the way we're playing.' Tonight I went in and got into them real bad because they were playing like they thought they could just put on the uniform and play. To their credit, they came out and played a hell of a second period."

If Parker gave his team somewhat mixed reviews, it was

a giddy night for BU fans, who showed some creativity in starting an unlikely new chant: "Er-ic Gry-ba!" "It was cool; it was funny," Gryba remembers. "You don't hear too many people chanting for defensive defensemen. No idea why they did it."

CROWD PLEASERS

While the atmosphere at Agganis varies considerably depending on whether classes are currently in session, there is no doubt that it's a blast to watch games there when the place is rocking. The BU band is a fixture behind the home net, exuberantly blasting out everything from "Hey Ya" to "Bohemian Rhapsody" with several dozen musicians standing up to play during almost every break in the action. When the Terriers score in bunches, the opposition must hate hearing the same celebratory song playing over and over again.

Brian Zive, a.k.a. Sasquatch, is a hirsute Terrier alumnus who frequently rouses the crowd by ripping off his shirt and baring his hairy torso, exhorting the crowd while the band runs through "Iron Man", his theme song. He usually waits until around the midway mark of the third period before displaying his pelt, and Sasquatch sightings are generally more probable during a tight game when he senses that the crowd may need to lend a hand. Some women avert their eyes from the shaggy sight, but most everyone loves it.

Swearing is forbidden at Agganis, requiring fans to be a little more creative in their choice of chants. Fortunately for Parker, the profanity police don't monitor his comments behind the bench. On opening night for the arena in January 2005, I told Parker that fans could really hear everything much louder from the ice surface. In response, Parker quipped, "I hope not some of things that *I* was saying."

Given that Brandon Yip is an Asian-Canadian player, the fans responded to his numerous penalties by facetiously chanting "You're a racist" at the referees. Fans unfamiliar with that ritual sometimes seemed a little outraged by it, not realizing that it was not intended as a serious accusation. For Yip's part, he always found it highly amusing. "When I first heard it, I started dying laughing. I couldn't even hear it at first, but when I did I thought it was really funny. It was a good chuckle; I didn't mind at all."

In recent years, the student section has featured a pair of fans who dress up respectively as The Hot Dog and Jesus. As this always invites quizzical reactions, they are usually quick to tell fans the rationale: "Not everyone believes in Jesus, but everyone believes in the hot dog."

While researching this book, I was amused but not surprised to see that this quirky pair has their own blog. As you might expect, it's just a tad partisan, as they apparently are diehard followers of *all* Terrier sports. Yet there are some truly hilarious posts. One asks "What can't Gryba do?" as a headline above a fishing trip photo in which the defenseman holds a catch that is almost as large as Joe Pereira. Below the photo, The Hot Dog answers his own question: "Nothing. The answer is Eric Gryba can do everything, ever."

No wonder Gryba marvels at the experience of being a Terrier athlete. "I try to explain to my buddies back home what it's like here, the atmosphere at the games," Gryba says. "It's not going to happen in the pros. You don't hear many defensive defensemen getting chants in the pros. We're so sheltered here. When you look at it, everything's paid for if guys are on scholarship—our housing, our locker room, our dining halls with unlimited food. Going to the pros you have to look out for yourself. Here we're so taken care of."

If the chanting for Gryba seemed random to him, Parker believed that it was completely fitting. "He was immense this weekend," Parker said, indicating this his performance measured up to his impressive size. "He was terrific with the puck, terrific banging people, terrific competing, terrific killing penalties. Because of the lineup back there, he and Straity don't get a lot of recognition. Everyone has a role to fulfill on the team, and he fulfills his as well as anybody."

TRADING PLACES

Speaking of Strait, his injury on Saturday was the one black cloud from the weekend for a team that had been almost untouched by serious injuries all season. "It sucked," Strait says. "I remember I played horrible on Friday night out at UMass, and I was so pissed off. My parents came down to talk, and I didn't want to talk. I was just 'Hi, I'll see you later.' On Saturday, I got out there, felt good. First period I was really happy with how I was playing, happy with the score because we were up. The second period had just started, and I came around the net—didn't see the guy and got blindsided. My leg went behind me, and right when I went down, I said, 'This ain't good.'"

Strait walked down the runway, engaging in some serious wishful thinking. He hoped it was just a stinger and told trainer Larry Venis that he would give it a spin. "This is just a throwaway game, Bri, we don't need you to hurt it anymore," Venis told him. By then, the trainer had already told David Quinn that Strait was done for the night. It was a medial collateral ligament injury, and Strait would end up out of action till the Hockey East semifinals. Steve Smolinsky would have to step into the lineup once again.

As the team adjusted to this new reality, a little comedy relief emerged the following week. Coming off a satisfying four-point weekend against UMass, Nick Bonino got some interesting news from his family advisor. Bonino had originally been drafted by the San Jose Sharks, and prevailing rumors indicated that his rights might be dealt to another team with the NHL trading deadline looming on March 4. The team was practicing at Walter Brown Arena that day, and Bonino had received no word about a deal when he left his phone behind at 2:40 to go to practice. Given that the deadline was 3 p.m., it appeared that he was staying put.

By the time practice ended, Bonino returned to his locker and found eight missed calls. One text message from his advisor tersely announced "traded." He took calls from the Sharks and his new team—the Anaheim Ducks—and tried to make sense of it all. "It was interesting," Bonino says. "It doesn't happen much to college players. I got drafted so late, and a lot of teams didn't know much about me until I got on a bigger stage. I got a call the day of the trading deadline from my family advisor, and he told me I might get traded but that it wasn't anything bad—it means another team likes you."

His teammates ribbed him about it, calling him "Suitcase" for a few days. In a way, the deal seemed fitting. Along with Brandon Yip and Steve Smolinsky, Bonino frequently played an Xbox game called "Halo 3". Now he could mull the possibility of playing "Halo" some day in a city known for the Angels.

TITLE ROLE

Now just one weekend remained in the regular season, and, for once, the Terriers did not have their destiny in their hands with a title at stake. Northeastern still owned a one-point edge in the standings. While the Huskies had to face always-dangerous Boston College twice over that last weekend, they also had much more at stake than the Eagles, who were locked into the No. 6 seed for the playoffs regardless of the weekend's results.

Still, opportunity appeared to knock on Friday night when BC held a 1-0 lead over Northeastern into the game's final half-minute, only to have Randy Guzior score an extra-attacker goal to tie the game up with just under 26 seconds to play. Then Steve Quailer scored in overtime for the Huskies in front of their jubilant fans, and Northeastern still appeared to have a solid grip on claiming the title as outright regular-season champions.

BU kept pace with NU by thumping Providence by a whopping 8-2 margin. It was Senior Night for the Friars down at Schneider Arena, but it was a Terrier senior who earned the highest accolades of the evening. Brandon Yip had a hat trick and an assist to lead the way, while linemate Nick Bonino showed no ill effects from his recent trade, notching two goals and three assists of his own.

Freshman goalie Alex Beaudry might have stumped BU back in January, but he looked decidedly mortal on this night, giving up seven goals on 24 shots before getting pulled. Perhaps it was too late to pull out a regular-season championship, but at least the team could feel good about having all cylinders firing going into postseason play.

Then the nearly unthinkable happened on Saturday night. Northeastern picked a terrible time to play one of its poorest games of the season, coughing up three power-play goals to lose at BC, 4-1. "It just stinks," Northeastern coach Greg Cronin told USCHO's Jim Connelly afterwards. "To go from start to finish in first place and play like we did tonight, it just stinks."

Due to fortuitous scheduling, BU's final game was not till the next afternoon against Providence. Therefore, the Terriers could go into the game with the added boost of knowing that a win would give them the regular-season championship. "When Northeastern lost that night, it kind of picked everyone up. We knew it was a great opportunity to win that championship as well," John McCarthy recalls.

The game started late, as Providence's drive up to Boston seem to symbolize the Friars' entire season. "We got a flat tire on the way on the Mass Pike coming in, about five miles from the rink here, and I actually had to laugh," Friar coach Tim Army said. "Usually I wouldn't laugh, but it was just the way it was supposed to be, I guess. It's just been one of those years. We'll grow from it, and we'll learn from it."

Although the game now mattered much more than it might have, the coaching staff never wavered from the plan of giving Grant Rollheiser one more turn between the pipes. "With Rollheiser, he loses to Providence [earlier in the semester] and I play him for the league championship with Jack's blessing," Geragosian says. "This is important for seeding and for the flag. We played Rollheiser because he stepped it up and played well off the bench against UMass. We gave him an important situation."

If the Friars had a flat tire, though, it was BU that looked flat early on. Notwithstanding the supposed incentive of Northeastern losing the night before, Parker deemed his players to be "half-asleep" in the first period. It proved to be tougher sledding at home than it had been on the road on Friday night, but they won it. With Rollheiser looking solid in goal and Popko, Saponari, and Higgins lighting the lamp, the Terriers shut out Providence 3-0 and found themselves in first place for the first time—on the last day of the season.

"It took us an extra day in the season to catch [Northeastern], and we've only lost one game since November," Parker marveled afterward, referring to the Huskies' excellent showing in league play throughout the year. "In some ways, it would have been nice if we were co-champions because we both deserved it. They've had a heck of a season. I'm hoping we get a chance to see them later on."

Tim Army made what turned out to be a fairly prophetic comment at the press conference. "They're very, very good," Tim Army said of BU. "I said the other night that in my four years here, we've played some really good teams. Last year BC won the national championship, but I think this is the best team I've seen. They're deep at every position."

Although the captains were able to hoist yet another

trophy, there was no sign of irrational exuberance in the post-game press conference. "It's nice," Terrier co-captain Matt Gilroy said about claiming the top spot in the league, sounding more like he was referring to kissing his sister. "We worked all year climbing up the league, and it's nice to be up top. But it ends pretty quick, and the most important season starts next weekend."

Parker agreed. "Fortunately for us, we've managed to accomplish our major goals for the regular season. And now we start over again. Everybody's equal."

Parker noted how Brown came into the ECAC playoffs that weekend with a 3-21-5 record and proceeded to beat Harvard in their first-round matchup, adding that he loved reading a quote from a Brown player who expressed the fact that his team had just as much a chance of winning the national championship as anyone. Most everyone in the media room laughed, but Parker wasn't trying to be funny. He completely agreed with the sentiment of that athlete.

It had been a very satisfying regular season for the Terriers. But all teams were equal in terms of wiping the records clean—not to mention the Terrier helmets, as all of the paw prints earned during the regular season were now removed as usual for the postseason. BU would have to prove that it was equal to the task of ending several teams' seasons. No matter how much talent a team may have, that is always a tough task to do repeatedly over the waning weeks of college hockey's highest-stakes games.

FINAL SCORE AT END OF PERIOD TWO:

Boston University Record: 16 Wins, 1 Loss, 3 Ties (27-5-4 for the season)
Goals: Boston University 86, Opponents 35 (BU 143, Opponents 69 for the season)
Championships: Denver Cup, Beanpot, Hockey East Regular Season (Four titles to date for the season)

THIRD PERIOD

Postseason:
Spring Semester

BEARS TO CROSS

As the No. 1 seed in the Hockey East quarterfinals, BU opened the postseason by hosting a best-of-three matchup against the No. 8 seed, the University of Maine. The 27-5-4 Terriers were a prohibitive favorite over the 12-20-4 Black Bears, but that would not necessarily mean much in an extremely competitive league. Back in 1998, a top-seeded Terrier team lost to Merrimack, a No. 8 seed. In 2004, an eighth-seeded BU team went out to Conte Forum and salvaged some respect by knocking off No. 1 Boston College. Still, few gave the Black Bears much of a chance to pull off the upset.

They would come much closer than anyone would anticipate.

In Friday night's opener, low totals of shots and goals as well as dueling goaltenders meant that Maine played just the kind of game they wanted to play.

Except for the final score.

In a sense, opening night of the Hockey East playoffs would be an almost eerie foreshadowing of the national tournament, as the No. 1 seed was the only favored team to win. So while it was the opposite of home sweet home for all of the other high seeds in Hockey East, BU did win but needed to rally to eke out a 2-1 victory over Maine. Colby Cohen and Kevin Shattenkirk led the way offensively, while Colin Wilson was the only Terrier forward on the scoresheet at all.

"My first thought is I was very, very impressed with the way the opposition played tonight," Parker said afterward. "I thought Maine played great. They did a great job killing penalties; we only got one for eight, and the only power-play goal we get is on a five-on-three. They did a fabulous job in front of their own net, and they kept pressure on us because of the way they changed their forechecks. They had different looks, and they executed very well.

"I thought we were somewhat lackadaisical at times, and then when we tried to turn it on we couldn't pull away from this club because they played so hard."

For Maine coach Tim Whitehead, it was a missed opportunity to notch a road win, and one had to wonder if an underdog could win such a series after not capitalizing on that chance. "It was a hard-fought game," Whitehead said. "Unfortunately, we came out on the wrong side of it, but I was proud of how our guys competed and played. We were pleased with how our guys were playing. We stuck to the game plan. We certainly had our chances to win it, and we defended pretty well."

The Terriers had the better of the chances for most of the first period. At 6:45, Wilson undressed Matt Duffy with a move but couldn't score on the subsequent shot. Maine's first chance came at 8:20 off a faceoff following an icing, when Keif Orsini threatened with a 12-foot backhander, only to have Kieran Millan split for a flashy glove snare.

Then Maine stunned BU by scoring a power-play goal with 22.1 seconds left in the period. Matt Duffy took a right-point slapshot, and Tanner House redirected it past

Millan for the surprising lead.

BU temporarily gained momentum at the five-minute mark of period two, when two minutes of possession in the Maine zone led to a power play. That didn't lead to a goal, but the Terriers finally tied it at 10:59. Colby Cohen passed to Colin Wilson behind the net, and the sophomore—now a Hobey Baker candidate—attempted to tee it up for Jason Lawrence in the slot. Lawrence fanned on the one-timer, but the puck went out to Shattenkirk at the point, and his high shot found the net.

The Black Bears played some of their best hockey early in the third, testing Millan repeatedly. BU slowly regained its composure, and Joe Pereira almost snuck one through a throng of players at 12:45.

Finally, a BU five-on-three power play made the difference—though the Terriers scored with just three seconds left on the two-man advantage. Wilson proved pivotal once again, nearly scoring on a back-door attempt before teeing it up for Colby Cohen with a cross-ice pass from the right-wing circle to the left-wing circle.

"Great pass by Wilson," Cohen said. "Just a one-timer: I was trying to go back to the side that Darling was coming from. Wilson has such good patience with the puck. He sends a perfect flat pass right in my wheelhouse. You've got to give him most of the credit on that play."

It wasn't over yet. Once Maine pulled Darling, Black Bear forward Gustav Nyquist—the team's leading scorer—very nearly tied it in the waning seconds. "We give up a three-on-one with 11 seconds to go because everybody's trying to get an open-net goal, and my defenseman's got no stick trying to get it out of the zone," Parker said. "They make a great play, and my goalie makes a fabulous save or else we're still playing."

"It wasn't a great effort by us, but in the same breath Maine had a really good game and probably deserved a better fate," Colby Cohen said. "But in the end, we found a way to win, and that's what good teams do."

"You've got to give them credit," Parker said of the Black Bears. "They came here to play the No. 1 team in the nation, and they certainly didn't make us look like the No. 1 team in the nation. They made us look very vulnerable and very even with them. I don't mean that we looked like the eighth team in the league: They looked like a terrific hockey team tonight in every area of the game... I was disappointed that we didn't play with more emotion, with more zip. We were very fortunate to get a W tonight."

The Terriers would not be so fortunate in game two. I, for one, thought that Maine likely would fold after coming close on Friday without getting rewarded. I couldn't have been further off the mark. When BU co-captain John McCarthy scored a shorthanded goal to make it 3-1 in the first period, it certainly looked like the game might be over.

In a sense, it was.

Maine had not won a game all season when giving up three goals or more. They were on a nine-game winless streak, facing a BU team that had a 17-game unbeaten streak and which had lost only once since November 22. Yet the Black Bears responded amazingly well to the gut check, rallying to score five unanswered goals to beat BU 6-3 to force a deciding game three in the quarterfinal series.

Standout freshman Gustav Nyquist led the way with two goals and an assist for the Black Bears, who also received two-point nights from Chris Hahn, Robby Dee, Tanner House, Matt Duffy, and Simon Danis-Pepin. Scott Darling made 29 saves for the Black Bears. Most strikingly, Maine went four-for-seven on the power play that night, while BU was skunked on five man advantages.

"Obviously, it was a completely different game than last night, and the outcome was different," Parker said at the press conference. "I didn't like the way my team played tonight but for different reasons. We played with a little more intensity and heart tonight, but they looked like the BU hockey team and we looked like somebody else. When it's four-for-seven on the power play, that's supposed to be us. We had some guys come back and play better tonight and some guys not play well. I thought as a group, our corps of defensemen had tough nights. We gave them some goals; we had some bad reads. We didn't do a good job handling the puck as well."

After the two teams combined for three goals in 60 minutes in game one, it took just over five minutes to match that total on Saturday night. Maine scored 42 seconds into the game when Steve Smolinsky, filling in for the injured Brian Strait, turned over the puck on his goal line, leaving Millan all alone against Gustav Nyquist and Chris Hahn, who ultimately converted it.

BU got that one back at 3:40 with the kind of gritty goal that Parker likes. Chris Higgins dug the puck out of the right-wing boards and slid it behind the goal line to Colin Wilson, who held off a defender long enough to center it to Brandon Yip for the one-timer and goal.

The Terriers took the lead during four-on-four play at 5:23. Luke Popko's forechecking helped Matt Gilroy snag a turnover and drive from the corner to the net. The puck was pokechecked away, but Popko batted it home.

An apparent backbreaker for Maine came at 5:23. Shorthanded, McCarthy disrupted a Maine rush, and Jason Lawrence fired the loose puck to McCarthy for the breakaway and goal. However, Maine got that one back on the same power play, just 26 seconds later. Nyquist collected the rebound of a Matt Duffy shot and roofed a backhander.

"I think the whole team just stepped up," Nyquist said. "I think everyone on the bench was excited to come back. We felt great on the bench, even though we were down 3-1. I'm just so proud of our team effort tonight. This was a great team effort and a very exciting game."

Just 21 seconds more elapsed, and Maine tied it. Keif

Orsini skated into the zone and fired an ordinary-looking wrist shot. Millan should have gloved it, but it caromed off his glove and trickled toward the goal line at about five miles per hour. It was very close, but referee Jeff Bunyon had a great vantage point and decisively signaled a goal. It went to video review, which gave no reason to refute the call on the ice. The goal marked the first time all season BU had yielded three goals in a period.

The teams took a breather from scoring for quite a while at that point, though BU still looked careless in its own zone, with defensemen struggling with turnovers and half-fanning on outlet passes. Finally, Maine regained the lead at 10:11 on another power play. Spencer Abbott took a shot from the left-wing circle to beat Millan low.

It still felt like BU might turn it on to pull out another win, but that never came close to becoming a reality the rest of the way. Nyquist made it 5-3 at 6:16 of the third on a gorgeous wrist shot from the right-wing circle, beating Millan high on the glove side.

The Black Bears basically sealed it at 11:04 when Millan couldn't cover a loose puck in the crease and Robby Dee knocked it home. Matt Gilroy had a great shorthanded chance off a faceoff at 14:30, but that shot went wide, and it proved to be the last gasp.

"The way they played tonight, they were the much better team," Parker said. "In reality, they probably should be going home right now and getting ready for the Garden because we stole one last night, and now they come back and beat us 6-3."

Afterward, I asked Parker about a bit of a paradox. On the one hand, as Colby Cohen had pointed out the night before, good teams find a way to win even when they aren't playing their best. Yet that also can mean that the team perhaps has been rewarded for the wrong behavior by getting some wins despite not playing all that well over the last few games.

"We've been on this slippery slope for a while," Parker

agreed. "You can't tell them 'You only tied; you only won by a goal.' You have to get slapped upside the head, and it will be interesting to see how we respond to that tomorrow night. If we get by tomorrow night, maybe this will be a good thing. If we don't get by tomorrow night, it will be because the better team came out and stuck it to us. We are not playing at the level we were playing at earlier, and we'd better make sure we get back to that."

In retrospect, getting "slapped upside the head" by Maine on that Saturday proved to be the best thing that could have happened to BU. The loss didn't cost the team anything except needing to play a third game in three nights, and the benefits turned out to be huge. Although the team had only lost one game since November at that point, they had sometimes slipped into the habit of playing just well enough to get by. Maybe they had started believing that they didn't need to play any better to continue winning.

For two nights in a row, a sub-.500 team had deserved to win more than they had, regardless of the talent differential between the clubs. Maine forced the players to swallow a tall pint of humility, and the loss reminded everyone that they would need to redouble their commitment to the Burn-The-Boats mentality.

The intensity returned for game three—as did the alternate white jerseys for the home team. The Terriers wore them on Friday night but switched to the regular home uniforms for Saturday. After losing, they quickly switched back to the alternate jerseys. They never switched, or lost, again.

If Maine was unlucky on Friday the 13th, the Black Bears had good reason to beware the Ides of March Sunday night. After outplaying BU for the first two games of the series, the Black Bears were trounced 6-2 by the Terriers. BU's second line led the way with six points, including a goal and an assist each for Nick Bonino and Brandon Yip. Kieran Millan looked sharp in the net with 24 saves after a shaky night on Saturday.

"In general, I thought we came out with a lot of energy and intensity in the first period," Parker said. "We came after them pretty good—scored right off the bat. I thought that the biggest goal of the game was our second goal. When they had scored to make it 1-1, we scored right after that. We answered pretty quickly and then answered again. Those two goals turned it around for us and gave us a lot of confidence."

Meanwhile, Maine coach Tim Whitehead was talking bull after the game. "It reminded me a bit of a bullfight," Whitehead said, making an amusing if wistful analogy. "Everyone's here, and they kind of know what's going to happen. Some people were hoping that maybe the bull might get the matador, but not tonight. The bull got a piece of him last night, and I guess that's why people come back to the games—you never know what's going to happen. We got close. They had a near escape the first night, and we got them the second night, but I thought the matador was very sharp and finished off the bullfight tonight."

After taking a beating Saturday, the Terriers didn't waste any time getting going with a goal 58 seconds into play. Co-captain John McCarthy carried the puck over the blue line on the left-wing side before dropping it to fellow senior Yip trailing the play. Yip crossed it to Colby Cohen entering the zone at the far point, and the sophomore defenseman unleashed a blistering slapshot that beat Maine goalie Scott Darling high on the glove side.

Soon it came to light that while the Terriers had dressed six defensemen, only five were playing regularly until the third period. Steve Smolinsky had made a few costly turnovers the night before, and Parker opted to rotate his five healthy defensemen with Brian Strait still out of the lineup with a knee injury. With Strait slated to return the following weekend, it appeared that Smolinsky's Terrier career likely would end as a healthy scratch.

Boston University coach Jack Parker typically claps when most of the crowd doesn't in order to ensure players are rewarded for doing the little things right. *(Photo: Dominick Reuter)*

Associate head coach David Quinn
(Photo; Dominick Reuter)

Assistant coach Mike Bavis
(Photo: Dominick Reuter)

Terrier Lineup for National Tournament Games

Left Wings

#15 John McCarthy (C)

#10 Chris Higgins

#12 Chris Connolly

#11 Zach Cohen

Centers

#13 Nick Bonino

#33 Colin Wilson

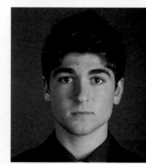

#9 Corey Trivino

#26 Luke Popko

Right Wings

#18 Brandon Yip

#21 Jason Lawrence

#27 Vinny Saponari

#8 Steve Smolinky

All Headshot Photos: Dominick Reuter

Left Defensemen

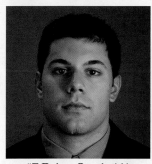

#7 Brian Strait (A)

#25 Colby Cohen

#5 David Warsofsky

Right Defensemen

#97 Matt Gilroy (C)

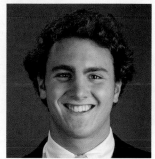

#3 Kevin Shattenkirk

#2 Eric Gryba

Goalie

#31 Kieran Millan

All Headshot Photos: Dominick Reuter

Other Terriers who saw game action:

#16 Kevin Gilroy (F)

#14 Andrew Glass (F)

#6 Joe Pereira (F)

#17 Victor Saponari (F)

#35 Grant Rollheiser (G)

Preparing for their first of 45 games, the Terriers huddle before the season opener against North Dakota. *(Photo: Dominick Reuter)*

Michigan State goalie Jeff Lerg made several acrobatic saves—including this one against freshman Chris Connolly—but couldn't stop the Terriers from winning the Ice Breaker Invitational. *(Photo: Dominick Reuter)*

Nick Bonino plays ping pong in the players' lounge, where the team often bonded in the first-rate surroundings. Bonino and Brandon Yip were acknowledged to be the team's top ping pong players in 2007-08.
(Photo: Dominick Reuter)

After opting to return to BU for his sophomore season, Colin Wilson led the Terriers in scoring in 2008-09 while making great strides off the ice as well.
(Photo: Dominick Reuter)

In the visiting locker room at Merrimack, Jack Parker poses with the team after recording his 800th win as a coach. *(Photo: Dominick Reuter)*

BU goalie Kieran Millan experienced some jitters during the first round of the Beanpot but was solid as usual when shutting down Ryan Ginand and Northeastern University in the championship game. *(Photo: Dominick Reuter)*

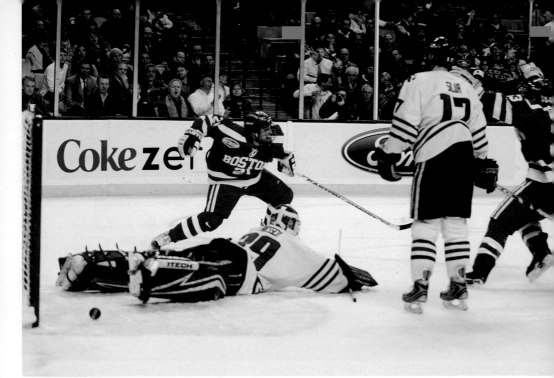

Jason Lawrence celebrates after scoring the eventual game-winning goal in the Beanpot champsionship. *(Photo: Dominick Reuter)*

Terrier captains John McCarthy, Matt Gilroy, and Brian Strait join head coach Jack Parker in accepting the weighty Beanpot trophy from Beanpot chairman Steve Nazro. *(Photo: Dominick Reuter)*

Brian "Sasquatch" Zive, a 1994 BU alumnus, is renowned for baring his hairy body to rile up the crowd at Terrier games. *(Photo: Dominick Reuter)*

Boston College shut down BU for the first 51 minutes of the Hockey East semifinal… until this goal by Zach Cohen began an outburst of the three Terrier goals in just 44 seconds. *(Photo: Dominick Reuter)*

Kieran Millan looked great with a 1-0 shutout of UMass Lowell in the
Hockey East championship game, denying Paul Worthington on this shot.
(Photo: Dominick Reuter)

The BU players pose with the Hockey East tournament trophy, their fifth title
of the season. *(Photo: Dominick Reuter)*

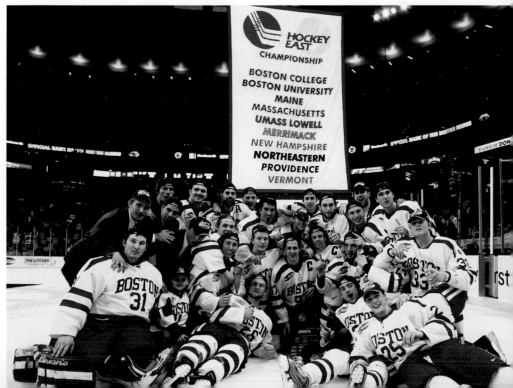

In the first game of the national tournament, Zach Cohen scored twice in BU's 8-3 romp over Ohio State. *(Photo: Gil Talbot)*

With an overdue trip to the Frozen Four on the line, Kieran Millan played a fantastic game in goal for the Terriers in the Northeast Regional final. Here he keeps his eyes fixed on the puck while Colby Cohen attempts to bat it away from Wildcat star James Van Riemsdyk. *(Photo: Gil Talbot)*

In the Frozen Four semifinals against Vermont, Chris Higgins gleefully savors the game-tying goal, which he banked off of Catamount defenseman Drew MacKenzie, who lies dejectedly in the net. *(Photo: Gil Talbot)*

After returning to BU for his senior year, Matt Gilroy ended up hoisting the 43-pound Hobey Baker Award as well as enjoying an opportunity to play with brother Kevin. *(Photo: Gil Talbot)*

After nearly being tossed off of the team during the previous offseason,
Steve Smolinsky wound up playing in the most exciting game of his life
and winning a national championship. *(Photo: Gil Talbot)*

Zach Cohen also avoided an ouster from the team in the spring and ended
up playing a key role for the national champions. His 13th goal was a lucky
one for the Terriers, as it was the first of two last-minute goals to tie the
national championship game. *(Photo: Josh Gibney)*

Defenseman Matt Gilroy leaps up on Nick Bonino after the centerman scored what Jack Parker calls the biggest goal in Terrier history. *(Photo: Josh Gibney)*

Screened by players in front of him, Miami goalie Cody Reichard never saw the deflected shot from Colby Cohen that gave BU the national championship in overtime. *(Photo: Josh Gibney)*

The team races off the bench to swarm Colby Cohen after the goal that won the championship. *(Photo: Josh Gibney)*

During the postgame celebration, a handful of Terriers doused coach Jack Parker with a bucket of Vitamin Water. *(Photo: Gil Talbot)*

Senior Brandon Yip puckers up for the national championship trophy. *(Photo: Gil Talbot)*

Jason Lawrence embraces Jack Parker's grandson, Jake Lachance. *(Photo: Gil Talbot)*

After winning it all, the Terriers finally explained the meaning of their warm-up shirts, which featured "Burn The Boats!" on the front and this image on the back. *(Photo: Dominick Reuter)*

Nick Bonino sneaks a peek at the big prize during the postgame press conference. *(Photo: Gil Talbot)*

Jack Parker and the players were astonished to see thousands of Terrier fans turn out for the Duck Boat parade and rally on Marsh Plaza after the team returned from Washington D.C. *(Photo: Dominick Reuter)*

Matt Gilroy parts the red sea of Terrier fans at Marsh Plaza, holding the grand prize aloft. *(Photo: Dominick Reuter)*

BU fired on all cylinders as the period progressed. Maine had a pair of shorthanded two-on-ones in the sixth minute, but otherwise the action was dominated by the Terriers. That almost changed at 12:19 when BU narrowly averted disaster. Jeff Dimmen drove at the net from the right-wing circle, and his sharp-angle shot got through Millan as the netminder went down. Cohen was the defensive hero this time, stopping the puck right on the goal line with his skate.

The Maine players raised their sticks, but a skate obstructed referee John Gravellese's view of the play. The video review proved inconclusive, and it was ruled no goal. The play was reminiscent of Cohen's game-saving save in game one of the previous season's quarterfinals against Lowell.

BU regained the lead with a gritty goal at 16:05. McCarthy outbattled a defender for a puck behind the goal line and slipped it to Bonino on the edge of the crease. The centerman fought off another Black Bear and backhanded a pass to Yip at the far side of the crease, where the winger knocked it in while falling down.

Twenty-nine seconds later, the Terriers kicked the Bears while they were down, thanks to the BU fourth line. Luke Popko teed up a David Warsofsky shot from the left point, and Joe Pereira redirected it slightly. The puck trickled through Darling to make it 3-1. It was the eighth time the team had scored two goals in under a minute over the course of the season.

BU's freshmen had been looking their best in quite a few games and finally joined the scoring party midway through period two. Chris Connolly rushed in on the right wing and tried to find Vinny Saponari crashing the net. The puck went through him, but Corey Trivino was hustling to the far post and tapped it in.

After another two minutes and change, it was 5-1. Matt Gilroy made a great read, getting the puck deep in his own end and firing a 100-foot pass off the boards to get it around a defender, sending Zach Cohen over the blue line for a breakaway resulting in a shot and score from the left-wing side.

If there was any tinge of doubt remaining, Bonino sealed it with a four-on-four goal at 15:04 of the second stanza. He took the puck away from Brian Flynn at the blue line for a breakaway, losing the handle near the net, only to have the puck drift through Darling.

It certainly looked like BU got a needed wake-up call after some rather ordinary play over the previous few weeks. "I think we knew it was win or go home [tonight]," Bonino said. "We played with urgency tonight and just pushed the tempo of the whole game. I think that was the key to get by Maine. We kind of thought we were going to the Garden Friday night, and that's not acceptable. The seniors called us out on it, and everyone buckled down."

ENDANGERED EAGLES

Now the Terriers would indeed go to the Garden, where they would attempt to pull off their first 30-win season since 1995-96 against archrival Boston College in the Hockey East semifinals. In the opening round, the No. 6 seed Eagles went up to UNH and managed to sweep the favored Wildcats. While BU had enjoyed success against its archrival all season, BC still owned the title of reigning national champions.

It's never easy to end a team's season, but it has to be harder when a team features many players who know what it takes to reach the big stage. Another bit of history for the Terrier seniors to ponder was how their freshman seasons had ended. Back in 2005-06, BU won the season series against BC and also beat BC in the Beanpot as well as the Hockey East championship game. Then, in the game that mattered most, the Eagles smoked the Terriers 5-0 in an NCAA Regional final, keeping a very good BU team from making the Frozen Four yet again. This would be an opportunity to avenge that high-stakes loss by finishing BC's season.

The teams had faced each other three times already over the season, but the Eagles saved their best for this last chance. They came out determined and had the first two chances, and then Brandon Yip continued his run toward the all-time Terrier record for penalty minutes in a season. Just 1:31 into the game, Yip was called for a five-minute major and a game misconduct for hitting from behind. That led to three more good chances for the Eagles just after the four-minute mark, but Millan and the BU penalty killers managed to survive that storm.

For the better of the first two periods, it was a scoreless defensive struggle. BU managed to get a few chances back by the end of the first, and Colin Wilson had a great opportunity from the left wing almost immediately after the opening faceoff in the second period. The Eagles countered at 1:38 with a two-on-one break, only to have David Warsofsky come up with a great defensive play to thwart the bid.

It looked as if BU might break on top at the midway point of the second period. Just five seconds into a power play, Vinny Saponari had an outstanding chance when the rebound of a Warsofsky shot landed on his stick. His shot was ticketed for the net, but Eagle sophomore John Muse made his best save of the night to keep the game knotted at zero.

Finally, BC took the 1-0 lead at 17:50 of the second frame. Brian Gibbons took a shot that Millan saved, but Ben Smith managed to knock the rebound out of midair and into the net.

Between periods, the players got in each other's faces, Matt Gilroy said afterward, challenging each other to take it up a notch. But two penalties early in the third period didn't help the cause. At the six-minute mark, the Terriers became a little overexcited with a possible shorthanded rush and ended up yielding an odd-man rush the opposite way. Clearly, the team had started to press. Yet I also had a feeling that came back to me repeatedly in the stretch: If they could score one goal, they might score two or more in a hurry.

Sure enough, the first snowflake led to a quick blizzard. It started with just 8:59 remaining in the third period, and it started with Zach Cohen—one of the guys who Jack Parker had come within the thickness of a skate blade from kicking off the team. When Yip was tossed from the game early on, Parker had put Cohen on the second line with Nick Bonino and John McCarthy. "The first period, here and there we both had our chances," Cohen recalls. "The second period, they had a lucky bounce, knocked the puck out of the air for a goal. And we were just not going to let that happen again as we had in the previous years."

With BC tiring with the puck in the corner at the end of a long shift, Cohen stunned the crowd with a move reminiscent of his childhood idol. "Jaromir Jagr was my favorite player for awhile because of how big he is and how he protects the puck," Cohen says. "This year I'd say Dustin Byfuglien for the Black Hawks because he's down there and nobody can take the puck away from him. That's what I just love to do—just getting down in the corners and then get open for shots."

Cohen made a move that would make Jagr or Byfuglien proud. "I think Nick got it in deep, and Johnny went after it in the corner, then I went in to support him," recalls Cohen. "Johnny hit a guy against the boards, and the puck squeaked through his legs. I picked it up off the wall and came out through the slot."

Cohen wanted to pass, but the BC defense left him alone to stickhandle unmarked across the slot toward the far post. "Bonino was up high for the outlet, and the defenseman stayed back with Bonino instead of coming to me so I couldn't pass to him. I brought it out, and Muse was playing close to the post. So I faked a backhand,

Muse went down, and I brought it all the way over and put it in."

"Every guy on this team contributed," Chris Higgins says. "You see a guy like Zach Cohen who played on the fourth line. He had skill, but at the same time the coaches saw him more as a gritty player. And he had 13 goals this year and some huge goals in the Hockey East semifinal against BC and obviously against Miami. When you see a guy like that score a big goal, it definitely sparks the rest of the team. He won the Most Improved Player award this year, and he definitely deserved it. He proved to be a big-time player who can score clutch goals and mostly from our fourth line at that."

"Zach Cohen must've beat one of our guys coming out of the corner deep on the side there," BC coach Jerry York said of the goal. "We almost got off the ice. It was an icing situation. We were trying to make a change, so we were a little tired off that faceoff."

Twenty-one seconds later, BU dazed the Eagles by seizing the lead. McCarthy fed the puck out to the left point, where Brian Strait—playing his first game in weeks and never an offensive threat—fired a shot that fluttered past the screened goalie to make it 2-1.

While the announcer struggled to catch up with the scoring, the Terriers buried a third goal just 23 seconds after their second to leave the Eagles reeling. On this one, similar to Cohen's goal, Colin Wilson dug the puck out of the right-wing corner and skated over with it to beat Muse.

The Terriers had one-upped their usual penchant for scoring two goals in under a minute by lighting the lamp *three* times in just 44 seconds total. That turned out to be a record in the Hockey East tournament, beating Maine's feat of scoring three goals in a 1:01 span against Lowell back in 1990. "It was pretty nuts," Cohen says. "You don't see two goals in one minute very often, so three was pretty wild."

Weirder still, BU scored its three goals on just four third-period shots. Go figure. Most importantly, though, McCarthy believes that these goal spurts reflected on how the team's character had evolved. "This is what we had been lacking in previous years—that killer instinct. Once we had a team against the ropes, we were going to finish them off. That was a big part of our success this year: We didn't let teams hang around."

BC got one back, but the three goals held up, and BU advanced to the league championship game with a 3-2 win. "BC played solid that game," McCarthy recalls. "Their goalie was playing well up to that 44 seconds; they were playing well defensively, and they were buzzing us a bit. That was the fourth time we played them this year, and it was the best they played against us all year. But Coach Bavis says all the time that great teams win even when they don't play great. We didn't play great that night, but we still found a way to win. We already knew that about our team, but it was another instance when we showed that."

At the subsequent press conference, I asked Jack Parker if he had an explanation for the outburst of three goals in one period. "El Niño?" Parker responded, and the media roared with laughter. "You think I could explain that?"

Months later, Parker wanted me to know that his line was not original. Over a decade ago, NHL star Brendan Shanahan facetiously blamed his scoring slump on El Niño, a meteorological phenomenon caused by temperature fluctuations in the tropical waters of the Pacific Ocean. El Niño has been blamed for droughts, floods, and various other climate disturbances across the world. That night, however, was the first time that those temperature anomalies have been associated with the outcome of a college hockey game. We ended up with a sudden rise in pressure, a flood of scoring, and a drought when it came to BC's postseason chances.

Sure sounds like something we can blame on El Niño.

Meanwhile, the night's other Hockey East semifinal also provided its share of sudden plot twists. After falling behind to Northeastern 2-0, UMass Lowell rallied to tie the game with an extra-attacker goal with just 19.9 seconds left in regulation before beating the Huskies in overtime.

It would turn out to be a tune that would become a broken record throughout the postseason.

NOTHING DOING FOR LOWELL

Parker and his staff turned their attention to a strategy for the championship game, cognizant of the fact that the River Hawks were playing not only for a league title but their sole chance for a berth in the national tournament. While studying game film of the River Hawks, Parker found their recent tactics somewhat bemusing. "Lowell is a difficult team for us to match up against because of the way they play," Parker says. "They do not let you forecheck. They just go get the puck and fire it into center ice with this ridiculous catchable pass rule."

I tell Parker that I don't understand the catchable pass rule.

He chuckles ruefully. "It's a crowded bus—nobody does. The catchable pass rule is a way for the referee to be able to wave off icing. If it was catchable, well why didn't he catch it then? It's a ridiculous statement.

"I got a game film of Lowell playing RIT, and I thought I was at a tennis match. The camera was almost at center ice. This is what would happen: The other team dumps it in, and the Lowell defenseman would pick it up. Without stopping, he would roll around the other side of the net and fire it indirectly off the boards to a guy standing at the red line who tipped it for Lowell—so they could forecheck, they thought. But the RIT goalie stopped it, and the RIT defenseman picked it up and fired it up to their wing, who tipped it in. This happened like six or seven times during the course of the game."

At this point, Parker intently shifts his head from left to right repeatedly, as if he's watching the action from center court at Wimbledon. "There's no time of possession for either team. That style is a way to negate a team from putting pressure on you on the forecheck or even with turnovers in center ice. There are no turnovers. You never have the puck, though, unless you go forecheck them.

"This has nothing to do with skill. Lowell has some of the best puck-handling defensemen in the league, but they choose to take advantage of that rule. Because of that, they take away a lot of the good things that we can do."

The River Hawks did exactly that for much of the championship game. There were enough raindrops to foreshadow a downpour of goals. It never happened, thanks primarily to Kieran Millan. The freshman denied Jonathan Maniff on a great backhander at 7:30 of the first, then stopped Michael Budd on the rebound. Seconds later, Nick Monroe had another strong backhand bid, followed by two River Hawks taking whacks at the rebound of a Steve Capraro shot a minute later.

The shots may have favored BU 14-12 in the first period, but I had the scoring opportunities as 5-2 Lowell. Yet the Terriers emerged with the 1-0 lead, thanks to a goal just 1:22 before the first intermission. John McCarthy shot from a sharp angle on the glove side of Lowell goalie Nevin Hamilton, and the puck hit the far post before caroming out into the crease, where Brandon Yip buried it, slipping the puck between the skates of UML defenseman Barry Goers.

That goal stood up all night. Not easily, though. Kory Falite had two good power-play chances in the second period, and generally the River Hawks just outworked the favored Terriers. Lowell very nearly tied it up during a wild scrum at 10:38 of the second period. With a good half-dozen players in or around the crease, a scramble ensued. The net went up off its moorings and came down again, and a whistle should have been blown at least twice. Finally, the puck went in the net, and *then* the whistle blew at last. The play went to video review.

"The referee was stuck between a rock and a hard place," Parker says. "He didn't blow the whistle; he should have blown the whistle three times, but he didn't, bottom line. So they went upstairs. All the guy upstairs had to say was the net was off, no goal. Because the minute the net is off the moorings—if it's dislodged at all, even temporarily—the rule now is that there's an automatic whistle, and there can be no goal after that. There should have been a whistle when he lost sight of the puck. But the guy upstairs didn't help him out at all. He said, 'No goal—the whistle had blown' when the whistle had not blown.

"So if I was Lowell, I would have been really ripshit about that explanation. But it still should've been no goal because at three different times the whistle should've blown, and one of them you could check—when the net was off. It was absolutely the right call, but it put the referees on the ice in a bad light. If they had told Lowell that it was no goal because the net was temporarily off the pins, that would've been a lot easier to accept than it was no goal because they blew the whistle."

Before the last period, the captains told the coaches that they wanted to address the team privately. "We were just like, 'Guys, we're one period away from another championship,'" Matt Gilroy remembers. "We went through what we'd done, what we'd been through as a team and said that there is no way that Lowell is going to take this away from us. Coming from us—Johnny and Straity and me—it means a lot more. Coach can get up there and rant and rave and light some guy up, but when your peer is ranting and raving and *he* cares that much, that means a lot more than one of the coaches coming in there and giving it to us. Guys responded to that."

That proved to be the case. BU played better, finally, over the last 20 minutes but couldn't put away the pesky River Hawks. "We became frustrated that game, wanting to make a bigger play or smarter play," Parker says. It came down to the last several ticks, and it looked entirely possible that Lowell might pull off their third extra-attacker tie in their last four games when their leading scorer Scott Campbell had a great bid with four seconds left. Terrier Nation held its collective breath when Campbell managed to get the puck all alone on the doorstep. Nothing doing.

"Part of the heritage of being a BU hockey player is playing in big games from the very beginning," said River Hawk coach Blaise MacDonald, who happened to be the Terriers' associate head coach when BU last won it all in 1995. "When you bring in Michigan State and North Dakota early in the year, and you bring in Michigan, he's played in a lot of big games.... He looks like Cool Hand Luke in there; nothing seems to faze him or rattle him."

MacDonald's next comment alluded to the fact that today's players often opt against wooden sticks in favor of those made of a composite of fiberglass, carbon fiber, aluminum, and other materials. It made for a welcome departure from a worn expression. "The puck jumps to our best player's stick with four seconds left, and he got a lot of composite on that. That was a big save, and he looked really cool doing it. That's what good goalies do."

Weeks after the season ended, Millan talks about how he once bore no resemblance to Cool Hand Luke on the ice. "I feel that I'm a better goaltender now. I think it's 95 percent mental; the rest is just some little things technically. I used to have a hot temper, if you can believe it. In juniors, if a guy took a shot and it went in, I took it personally. I didn't work for things. If I let in a couple of goals early, I'd get pulled. I would never complete the game; I couldn't just battle back like I did this year."

In general, the team's freshmen had a terrific season, but David Quinn—the team's primary recruiter—feels that Millan exceeded expectations more than any of the other rookies. "He had a great first year in juniors, but the first half of his second year he really struggled. We were wondering if maybe he would need to take another year, or if he'd be good enough. So we went out and actively recruited Rollheiser, and right around then Millan's game turned around big time. He had a great second half; he had a great playoffs. We thought he was going to be good, but…

"He's very calm. He's found that line: He's not lazy, but he's pretty damn close to it. He's found that zone of calmness, efficiency, and athleticism, but he doesn't waste any energy or any movement."

Once again BU enjoyed the heft of another formidable piece of hardware, as the players paraded the Hockey East tournament trophy around the ice at the Garden. In addition to the win representing the team's fifth title of the season, it was only the Terriers' second league championship since 1995, and Parker always describes it as one of the toughest to win.

The only bad news was that winger Joe Pereira managed to injure himself on a truly fluky play. Skating around the Lowell goal, he somehow caught his stick in the netting. His abdomen absorbed the force of the breaking stick, and he needed to be hospitalized with an injury to his spleen. It was touch-and-go as to whether surgery would be required. Regardless, the "Bulldog" clearly was done for the season and would have to miss the national tournament.

SELECTION SUNDAY

Speaking of which, the team met in the video room the following morning to watch the selection show for the national tournament. The mood was happy and loose. By then, both Matt Gilroy and Colin Wilson had been named as two of the ten finalists for the Hobey Baker Award, given annually to college hockey's best player. Actually, the exact criteria are as follows:

- Candidates must exhibit strength of character both on and off the ice.

- Candidates must contribute to the integrity of the team and display outstanding skills in all phases of the game.

- Consideration should be given to scholastic achievement and sportsmanship.

- Candidates must comply with all NCAA rules: be full-time students in an accredited NCAA college or university; and complete 50% or more of the season.

As the ESPN commentators debated who should receive the top individual honor, one player shouted out "Matt Gilroy!", but commentator Barry Melrose favored Wilson. It was an interesting debate to ponder. Playing on the nation's No. 1 team would help both players in the voting. Melrose liked Wilson because he viewed him as the most talented player on the best team. However, a counterargument easily could be made. Gilroy was the co-captain of the team, a terrific two-way player, and he had said no to many enticing offers to turn pro in order to return to his team and play with his brother.

Of course, Wilson declined the opportunity to go pro as well, though his circumstances were different in that he could only negotiate with the team that drafted him. Another factor could be Gilroy's personal story—the reason for his wearing of No. 97, and how he came to BU as a walk-on before reaching stardom and now was on the verge of a previously unthinkable professional career.

The more urgent matter at hand was the team's draw for the national tournament. As the No. 1 seed, some expected the Terriers would draw their complementary partner in the 16-team tournament. Bemidji State was the No. 16 seed. However, a BU-Bemidji State matchup would force a game between two Central Collegiate Hockey Association teams in another regional game, and the selection committee justifiably seeks to avoid that. As a result, BU drew the No. 15 seed, Ohio State. After the season, Mike Bavis told me that he was happy to get the Buckeyes instead of the Beavers, worrying that the Terriers—rarely lacking in confidence—might overlook a team from a smaller conference.

That made sense to me. Once you looked past Ohio State's impressive 23-14-4 record, it was clear that this was a talented but young team that also had struggled in the stretch, going 7-8-3 in their last 18 games. Then again, Michigan State came into the 2007 tournament with a similar season record and a 4-5-1 mark in their previous ten games— yet they proceeded to run the table for the national title.

As soon as the selection was announced, I handed Parker a printout from US College Hockey Online's page summarizing Ohio State's schedule and results. He scrutinized it and intermittently made cautionary comments to the assembled team: "Hey, these guys beat Notre Dame, you guys... They beat Miami... They beat Michigan."

Clearly, the coach wanted to make sure that his confident team didn't look beyond its first opponent. Parker then double-checked the game's starting time with a few of us and clearly was pleased that it would not be an early-afternoon game up in Manchester, New Hampshire.

PASSING THE BUCKEYES

With the field in place, the next issue to face was the matter of who would replace Pereira in the starting lineup. When I first asked Parker at the selection show, he was noncommittal but noted that Andrew Glass was not an option due to a concussion. In my mind, that left Kevin Gilroy and Victor Saponari as the only alternatives, as they were the only other players to see action at forward all season. Either would be a great story, given that each would have the chance to join his brother in the lineup for the biggest games of their lives.

However, another great story emerged instead. "When

Joey got hurt, at first I thought that Kev or Vic or one of the other guys might get in," recalls Steve Smolinsky. "Then Yipper or one of my other roommates said, 'Maybe they'll put you back up on forward.' I kind of brushed it off because I'd played defense all year. Then when I went to practice, Coach pulled me aside and said, 'Listen, we're going to try you at forward this week, see how it works out.' That was the weekend before the Regionals. He said, 'Are you nervous at all? Are you comfortable with that?' I said, 'Absolutely.' I was excited because I wanted to play. So he threw me in there, and I wondered all week if I was going to be able to stay in there. Thankfully, I did."

With that, a guy who almost saw his Terrier career end unceremoniously the previous spring would be able to go out playing in the most exciting games of his life.

Before the team left for New Hampshire, they were surprised with a special video that Joe Pereira made from his hospital bed. "It's the Bulldog!" he announced with a big, goofy grin before delivering a motivational message. "That was cool to see that before we left for the NCAAs," Gilroy recalls, chuckling. "Joey was saying, 'Get the job done.'"

"It lightened everyone up," McCarthy says. "It was good because it let guys know he was okay; he had a pretty serious injury."

In the national tournament, the teams are divided into four regional sites with four teams at each. Two of the Regionals start on Friday and finish on Saturday, while the other two begin on Saturday and end on Sunday. By Sunday night, the 16 teams would be whittled down to a quartet, all bound for the Frozen Four in Washington, D.C.

It would turn out to be the least predictable tournament in the history of college hockey.

Whether a team started playing on the Friday versus the Saturday may seem irrelevant. This year, though, BU reaped a benefit by being able to watch the first night's results before commencing action on the second day. Two of the four top seeds in the tournament played on Friday, and they both went down. Air Force received fantastic goaltending from Andrew Volkening, who stopped all 43 shots to lead the Falcons over heavily favored Michigan by a 2-0 score. Meanwhile, Miami outshot and outplayed Denver, ousting the Pioneers with a 4-2 win.

Even the other two games provided insights as to what surprises might be in store for an unsuspecting opponent... as well as the shape of things to come in the tournament in general. The University of Minnesota Duluth rallied with two extra-attacker goals in the last 40 seconds to beat Princeton, scoring the game-tying goal with just 0.8 seconds left before winning in overtime. In the fourth game, Vermont managed to beat Yale, a mild favorite partly due to the fact that the East Regional was in Bridgeport, Connecticut.

Altogether, the Terriers absorbed plenty of sobering news while waiting to play. "Playing Ohio State, our mentality was that we were treating it like a championship game," Colin Wilson says. "We had seen upsets in the past with Holy Cross against Minnesota and this year with Air Force and Bemidji. Seeing those two teams win, we were going, 'We have to win here; we're going to have to do whatever it takes.' So we took them very seriously—more serious than any other No. 1 seed took a 4 seed. That allowed us to go out there and have an offensive blowout—scoring goals and making the right plays."

Indeed, BU's opener proved to be the most lopsided game in this year's tournament, an 8-3 blowout that basically was over before the midway point of the second period. In fact, when Nick Bonino scored the team's first goal at 8:49 of the first period, recent history might have suggested that the game was on its way to being over right then. After all, the Terriers came into the national tournament with an astonishing 21-0-3 record in games in which the sophomore had scored at least one point this season. When Bonino has been skunked on the scoresheet, BU held a far more earthly 10-6-1 record to that point.

On that goal—a power-play tally—Brandon Yip passed from the right point to Bonino in the face-off circle on the same side for the shot and the goal. Forty-five seconds later, the Terriers scored again, marking the 11th time all season that they had scored twice in under a minute. Bonino factored in that goal as well, racing in with the puck on a two-on-one with Jason Lawrence. The centerman drew the defender toward him before slipping a last-second pass to Lawrence for a backhand shot that trickled past OSU goalie Dustin Carlson.

Less than four minutes after that, Zach Cohen snagged a loose puck in the right-wing circle and buried a high shot to make it 3-0. The Buckeyes tried to fight back at 15:20, but Millan stoned C.J. Severyn when the freshman crashed the net for a great chance. It would was Millan's most important save of the game.

After a lull in scoring, BU put the game away with two goals in just over a minute early in the second period. On a delayed penalty at 5:57, Gilroy drove to the net before slipping to Corey Trivino for the tap-in goal. Then Bonino's line struck again at 7:01, with McCarthy and Bonino working the puck between the two of them to produce a shot. Carlson stopped that one, but Yip banged in the rebound for a 5-0 lead.

The teams traded three goals apiece the rest of the way—including a second goal apiece for Lawrence and Zach Cohen, as BU went on cruise control. On my way to the press conference, the team walked past me on their way to the locker room, clearly in high spirits. "That was a statement," one player said. Another took on the voice of a public-address announcer: "And now… the new record-holder in penalty minutes for a single season… Brandon Yip!" Several teammates snickered. Indeed,

Yip had drawn two minor penalties, ensuring that he had passed Doug Friedman's 1993-94 total of 112 minutes for the dubious title.

Did the coaches have a problem with Yip's record? "It wasn't for me," Mike Bavis says. "Coaches can have a tendency to stress over particular players who are taking penalties. Yip's effort from start to finish this year was just spectacular in terms of how hard he played and how hard he competed. The vast majority of his penalties were not cheap, selfish, retaliatory penalties. They were usually gritty, tough penalties."

CAT VERSUS DOG

The Terriers couldn't celebrate very long, knowing that they would have to face UNH the next day, playing in its home state. In the day's matinee game, the Wildcats had won a topsy-turvy thriller against North Dakota. UNH scored the first goal before falling behind 2-1. Then the Wildcats rallied to make it 3-2, only to surrender three straight Sioux goals to make it 5-3 North Dakota well into the third period. Amazingly, UNH got one back and then managed to tie it with 0.1 seconds left in regulation, sending the largely partisan crowd at the Verizon Center into pandemonium. It just took 45 seconds of overtime for the Wildcats to win it 6-5.

Under the circumstances, one could forgive the Wildcats for starting to believe that they might be a team of destiny. Frankly, BU would have preferred to play North Dakota in the Regional final. When you keep playing a team in your league, you don't have that invincibility. "When we played Ohio State, they were 'Oh my God, we're playing BU,'" David Quinn says. "When we're playing UNH or Vermont, we don't have that mystique. They're not afraid of us; they think they can beat us."

"UNH knew that they could beat us, and they had the bitterness of not making it to the Garden to motivate them," Mike Bavis says. "I thought that they were going to be a dangerous team."

And if the team had seemed loose and a little cocky after the Ohio State blowout, the mood became heavier as they started to perhaps overthink what it would mean to get to the Frozen Four for the first time since 1997.

In a way, it was ironic. So much had been made over the course of the year about what it had meant to be a BU hockey player over the history of the program. In fact, Mike Eruzione would be the latest Terrier legend to address the team before the UNH game, reprising the theme from earlier in the season. Players like John McCarthy had a deep appreciation of the BU legacy, and there is no question that the seniors' commitment to restoring Terrier pride had been a major factor in the team's reversal of fortune over the course of the last year. However, it also may have amplified the pressure that the team suddenly put on itself to be equal to that legacy by returning to the Frozen Four at long last.

Another consideration was being the No. 1 overall seed. Every team that fails to make the Frozen Four will go home disappointed over what might have been. Yet the sting is stronger for any team that is not only hoping to get there but fully expecting to do so.

"You could almost feel it," McCarthy says. "Guys were a little more uptight because [making the Frozen Four] had been a goal of ours all year long. We had had success up to that point. Especially when things weren't going that way, guys were saying 'We've got to do something here.'"

Over the years, whenever I've asked players or coaches about the impact of not winning a Beanpot, a league championship, or reaching some other yardstick of success for many years, they almost invariably discount the history as irrelevant. You usually hear clichés about how every year is different, how anyone can win it, and how no one cares about what happened in the past. Yet that is simply not true in terms of what's going through the minds of at least some players and coaches.

"It seemed like every year that there was more pressure because it had been so long since BU made it to the Frozen Four," McCarthy says. "It does carry over. It does. When your program isn't represented on the national stage, it does put pressure on each team. I was glad that we reset that pressure—now it's over, and the guys can just play."

But if some of the veterans were fretting about how much a win or loss would mean to the program, freshman Kieran Millan remained blissfully ignorant of all that history. After struggling with jitters in the opening of the Beanpot, Millan came into that enormous game with UNH in the perfect frame of mind. "I felt fine. I felt completely comfortable."

Millan's composure would be the difference that allowed BU to eke out a dramatic last-minute victory against a relentless UNH team that deserved a better fate. "We had the one-nothing lead," Millan says. "I thought I played really well the first two periods, then I got a little flat-footed and gave up a rebound. Going into the third period, I assumed that we'd win. That's what we'd done all season, so to assume otherwise would be crazy. We made some mistakes that caused turnovers. It wasn't so much them outplaying us. That's my job, covering up mistakes, because I'm the last line of defense, and it's my job to stop the puck."

There would be plenty of opportunity to do that. Early on, Millan was fortunate when James van Riemsdyk shot wide on a two-on-one break that was almost a three-on-one jump. That would set the tone for much of the game, as the Wildcats enjoyed countless odd-man rushes.

Mike Sislo had a great chance at 8:43, and Colin Wilson wisely took a penalty to nix it. On the subsequent power play, though, Bobby Butler almost made it 1-0, only to have Millan make a terrific leg save. Colby Cohen failed to clear it, and UNH got another chance.

Surprisingly under the circumstances, BU struck first.

At 13:44, another freshman rose to the occasion, as Corey Trivino knocked in a rebound off a faceoff for a huge goal. Like many freshmen, Trivino had struggled to produce earlier in the year. Various minor injuries kept sidelining him, and that might have been a double whammy as missing time also kept him from gaining experience and confidence. Now, though, he had just scored two of his six collegiate goals in the NCAA Regionals, so that was quite timely.

UNH had two more great chances in the last minute of the period. Sislo had another good shot that Millan struggled to squeeze at 19:17. Then a puck bounced off Chris Higgins in the neutral zone, and junior Peter LeBlanc raced in for another chance with five seconds left in the period. Somehow BU escaped into intermission with a 1-0 lead.

Much to the delight of the better part of the crowd, UNH tied it up at 5:52 of the second period. Butler did it. On another two-on-one break, LeBlanc took the shot from the left wing. Millan stopped that one, but then Bobby Butler put it home.

Physically, the teams battled throughout the period. Yip barreled over goalie Brian Foster, who took exception to that. Jason Lawrence and Phil DeSimone were hitting and jawing. Later, Paul Thompson hammered Smolinsky with a hit. Both teams continued to pound each other and get the occasional scoring chance, but UNH looked better than BU on both fronts. Zach Cohen did have a good bid on a wraparound at the 18-minute mark, but Van Riemsdyk batted the puck out of the air to clear it from the crease.

The third period proved to be agonizing for the Wildcats and their fans. Sislo hit a post during a power play at 5:53. LeBlanc had a great scoring opportunity at 8:20 but to no avail. Halfway through the period, Blake Kessel set up DeSimone for a possible goal, but the big sophomore couldn't get the stick on it. At 14:50, the Wildcats threatened with a three-on-one, only to have Colby Cohen make the clear. Meanwhile, the Terriers had only a couple of middling chances going into the last minute of play. Would Parker and UNH coach Dick Umile—great friends off the ice—once again face an overtime game in a Regional final that would send one team home and the other on to greater glory?

Not this time. BU finally mustered a flurry with about 50 seconds to play. Mike Bavis points out that Brandon Yip was the unsung hero. After setting a team record for penalty minutes a day earlier, Yip's superhuman effort led to the opposition drawing a penalty. "Before we score the goal, watch the play that Yip makes to draw the penalty," Bavis says. "It's unreal. He comes off of that wall and refuses to be covered, ends up finding Bonino in the slot, and Bonino gets hooked."

So the Terriers went on the power play with just over 45 seconds left, and Jason Lawrence scored the biggest goal of his life on an odd play with 14.4 seconds remaining to seal it. In reference to Argentinean soccer legend Diego Maradona—who got away with scoring the winning goal in the 1986 World Cup quarterfinals against England by knocking the ball in with his fist—I like to call Lawrence's game winner the "hand of God" goal.

With his back to the net low in the left-wing circle, Lawrence spied linemate Colin Wilson open at the far post with plenty of net next to him. When Lawrence wound up to pass, Wildcat forward Jerry Pollastrone saw exactly what Lawrence had seen. As the pass went across the crease, Pollastrone—a guy who grew up playing with Lawrence and Higgins from around the age of nine—dove in an attempt to break up the play.

"He was laying out, and it just seemed like a reaction thing," Lawrence says. "He saw the puck and tried to swat it and mis-hit it. I was definitely going over to Colin."

Parker shrugs off the suggestion that Pollastrone might regret the play. "Wilson was just standing there by himself, and Pollastrone knew it. If Pollastrone doesn't put it in the net, Wilson does."

Mike Bavis still marvels at how that forward line produced the goal. "We play probably a 'C' game, but when the game is on the line, Chris Higgins rolls high and doesn't just shoot it on net. He makes a poised play down to Lawrence, who makes a poised play by stepping up and trying to make a pass to Wilson. Time and time again, that group made a play that won a game, and it wasn't just by happenstance."

Bavis also believes that UNH's stretch of bad bounces and close calls might have started to wear on their psyche by that point in the game. "At the end of the game, we had the belief that we would win it, and they probably had some self-doubt. When you give a team the five odd-man rushes that we gave them, and they shoot wide or miss… You give a team like that so many chances, and you usually pay for it."

For UNH—a team known for fans throwing a giant fish on the ice after the Wildcats score their first goal in any home game—this game certainly was a big one that got away.

"They played well," Lawrence says. "Coach said it was probably their best game of the year, and I totally agree with him. They played us as well as any team, including Miami. You play against another team so many times and break down tape, know what your weaknesses are. They had a ton of odd-man rushes, and we were biting our fingernails."

"Of all those games [in the postseason], that's the one where I would say that our opponent really outplayed us," Jack Parker says. "That's the game that our goaltender stole for us. Territorially, we were much better off in the first period, but after they scored they took over the game and had the much better quality chances. We struggled getting the puck in their zone, and they never had any trouble getting the puck in our zone. So that was probably the most fortunate game that we won probably with the exception of the final game. We dodged a bullet there."

Parker also sensed that his usually confident team looked unusually jumpy that day. "I don't think there's any question that we were really uptight. Once they scored the goal, we were back on our heels the rest of the game. There's no question that there was that much more at stake for us than most teams trying to get to the Frozen Four. We were the No. 1 team in the nation; we were the best team all year. If we don't get to the Frozen Four, it's a lot different than if Air Force doesn't get to the Frozen Four."

For the head coach, the thrill of victory was outweighed by the relief over making it to the Frozen Four for the first time in 12 years—especially after a few of those narrowly missed opportunities. "There's no question there was a sense of 'Wow, we're going to the Frozen Four again after not being there for a long time.' And with good teams—it wasn't like we stunk all those years. I think it was great because the seniors had the experience of not going to the Frozen Four as freshmen when we had a great team. So I don't know if it was vindication or relief or a sense of fair play that these guys finally got to go, but it was good news that they finally got to the Frozen Four."

SOWING UNLIKELY SEEDS

The drama between BU and UNH was not the only memorable outcome over the course of Regionals weekend. On Saturday, Vermont managed to beat Air Force in a double-overtime marathon. It ended very strangely, as a Vermont shot somehow went right through the netting. Play continued for a good while until the next whistle, and the Catamounts experienced the odd sensation of jubilantly celebrating a Frozen Four berth only after a very lengthy video review.

Meanwhile, Miami pulled off another upset, as the No.

4 seed beat Minnesota Duluth 2-1 up in Minneapolis. The RedHawks had a younger team that had won far fewer games than their 2007-08 team, which had a tough-luck loss to Boston College in the Northeast Regional final.

The other bracket provided the biggest shockers of all. Trailing 2-1 to Northeastern, Cornell scored two goals in the last four minutes—including a game winner with 18 seconds left—to pull out a gritty 3-2 win. That set up the Big Red for a matchup with Bemidji State, as the No. 16 seed in the tournament had stunned Notre Dame, the No. 2 team in the nation, with a resounding 5-1 win.

Just in case anyone thought that result was a fluke, the Beavers followed that result with a 4-1 win over Cornell on Sunday to become the first No. 16 seed ever to reach the Frozen Four.

Altogether, the Frozen Four's teams now included the following seeds: No. 1 BU, No. 9 Vermont, No. 13 Miami, and No. 16 Bemidji State. You have to look at it as a tribute to how far college hockey has come in terms of parity, and I would guess that coaches of plenty of No. 1 and No. 4 seeds are going to be reminding their teams of this tournament for years to come—either as a cautionary tale or as a motivator.

CAPITAL GAINS

In the week and a half between the Regionals and the Frozen Four, there would be ample time to rest up and strategize. One interesting subplot emerged when both Wilson and Gilroy were selected to be two of the three "Hobey Hat Trick" finalists for the Hobey Baker Award. I saw Jack Parker around the time of the announcement. He was pleased to see his players make the cut but surprised that Air Force forward Jacques Lamoureux was not among that troika.

Parker saw Lamoureux as a compelling option for voters in more ways than one. The forward had scored 33 goals and 20 assists for 53 points in 41 games, and Air Force had just stunned Michigan in the NCAA tournament. Most strikingly, Parker noted that Hobey Baker himself had been a pilot, giving voters another argument in favor of Lamoureux. For the sake of Gilroy and Wilson, the Terrier coach was relieved to learn that the Air Force star was out of the running. Instead, Northeastern's Brad Thiessen rounded out the selections. The winner would be named on the Friday between the semifinals and championship game in D.C., adding even more interest for Terrier fans.

While practicing in preparation for the Frozen Four, Chris Higgins recalls feeling that the team was spending an inordinate amount of time on extra-attacker situations—just in case they needed to tie a game in the waning minutes or seconds. "You think, 'Oh, it's a small chance [that it will matter]'," Higgins says. "But we were fortunate that we worked on it and how to execute it. The coaches definitely helped us prepare for so many close games."

When working on six-on-five play, the coaches opted to use freshmen Chris Connolly and Vinny Saponari exclusively as the extra attackers with Bonino's line or Wilson's line. That seemed insignificant at the moment but led to a surprising twist in the championship game.

As the team prepared for the big trip to the nation's capital, Jason Lawrence recalls the team feeling confident and excited. Parker asked the club if they wanted to do any sightseeing to break up the routine while they were down there. "The guys just kind of collectively said no," Lawrence says. "We're down there to win a championship; we don't want any distractions."

For Bernie Corbett, the trip to D.C. provided vindication. During the previous June, the Terrier announcer had made one of his usual summer sojourns around the country, going to baseball games and rock concerts. In Chicago, he met up with a few former Terriers, including Jacques Joubert, captain of the 1995 national championship team. When Corbett gushed about BU's chances of going far in

2008-09, Joubert razzed him mercilessly. "He says this *every* year!" Joubert crowed. Now the team had made it to the Frozen Four, and Corbett reminded Joubert about his skepticism. "You haven't won anything yet!" Joubert retorted, though he would have to eat his words soon enough.

After the season, Parker raved about Washington D.C. as a Frozen Four site. "I still say it's the best venue and that they should have the national tournament there every year. Two reasons: it's central and easy to get to, and between games there's a million things you can do and they're all for nothing. It's unbelievable, and it's such a beautiful city. It's amazing that they hadn't had a national championship there in any collegiate sport."

I would settle for every four years—just like the presidential election—but I see his point. It's a neutral site for everyone. The Verizon Center is a first-rate facility. Best of all, though, are the many great attractions. When I wasn't covering hockey over my three days in the capital, I was down by the Potomac, walking through the Vietnam Memorial and the Lincoln Memorial as well as the many other sights of the Mall.

Another day I went to the Library of Congress and enjoyed a terrific tour of its architecture and collections. I also visited the fascinating and cleverly designed American Indian Museum as well as the Air and Space Museum. Wherever I went, I saw fans wearing college hockey jerseys, soaking up those same sights and dozens of others. The weather was mild, and transportation and lodging were reasonable. The whole long weekend was just a fantastic life experience—one I would love to repeat.

Beyond some informal walks around the monuments, though, the players focused on business. Yet the experience of just getting there was magical for them as well. "Just being at the Frozen Four was a great feeling, especially as a senior," Chris Higgins says. "You dream about that as a little kid and just to get there—the reality setting in was unbelievable."

As the top seed, the Terriers enjoyed the added benefit of setting up shop in the locker room of the NHL's Washington Capitals, who graciously vacated their clubhouse for the tournament. "Everyone talked about getting [star forward Alex] Ovechkin's locker," Higgins says. "They didn't have the nameplates up, so guys just went around trying to take a guess at the locker." In the end, a Verizon Center employee told them that Grant Rollheiser had landed the Russian superstar's stall.

Before the tournament, Jack Garrity, Jr. had contacted Parker in search of tickets for the action. The call gave Parker a brainchild. "I said, 'Jack, I don't get Harvard guys tickets. But if you can get your father up from Florida, who is one of the top five players ever to play for BU for sure, there will be two tickets under his name, Jack Garrity, Sr., at the door. But only under one condition—that you and your dad will come to one of our team meals. We've had former BU hockey players come talk to our guys all year, and it would be great to have a guy from the first BU team to go to a final four come be around the team."

On Wednesday night—after a practice that looked so sharp that the coaches cut it short, quitting while they were ahead—Parker told the team that Garrity would be there for the team meal. Going back to his playing days in the late 1940s and early 1950s, Garrity is still the team's all-time record holder for goals in a season (51) and points in a season (84), while sharing the record for goals in a game (seven) and points in a game (nine). When Parker introduced Garrity to the team at dinner, the Terrier players rose and gave the legendary forward a standing ovation. "When they did, Jack was almost crying," Parker says. "It was fabulous."

The next day, the puck dropped for the opening semifinal. After all of the exciting action thus far, the first game turned out to be rather anticlimactic. Bemidji State's

Cinderella story came to a close against Miami, as the RedHawks looked like a defensive juggernaut in shutting down the speedy Beavers to earn a decisive 4-1 win.

As that action unfolded, the BU players and coaches felt highly confident and motivated going into their game with Vermont. "Ordinarily, I wouldn't be happy to play a Hockey East team in the tournament," Parker says, and that certainly had been the feeling about UNH in the previous round. "It's a national tournament, and you'd rather play other teams rather than these guys again. But I was happy to be playing them for a couple of reasons. For one, sometimes the devil you know is better than the devil you don't know, and I thought we were the better team. I think the only reason why they had [swept us at home was because] they had been more thorough than us."

FULL HOUSE, FULL CIRCLE

Everything had come full circle for the Terriers going back to the disappointing end of their previous season. "Once the game started, it was a dream come true, playing on a nationally televised stage against a team like Vermont," Higgins says. "This year they were the only team that swept us, and last year they ended our season in the Hockey East semifinals, so we definitely wanted a chance to get some revenge. There was no better place than on a national stage in the Frozen Four."

Even with such a backdrop, the game still exceeded expectations and became an absolutely thrilling battle. BU looked strong in the first period. Colin Wilson set up David Warsofsky for a short-side attempt just 95 seconds in, and Zach Cohen got another shot on net at 2:50.

BU drew an early penalty to Kevin Shattenkirk but followed that almost immediately with a shorthanded rush by David Warsofsky that could have drawn a Vermont penalty but didn't. With the exception of a Vermont two-on-one break leading to a bid by Hobey

Baker nominee Viktor Stålberg, almost every early opportunity belonged to the Terriers.

At 10:55 of the first, BU had its first excellent chance when Jason Lawrence set up Chris Higgins's shot. Vermont goalie Rob Madore stopped that one, but BU took the lead just 24 seconds later. Shattenkirk shot from the left point, and Wilson—flashing the skill that landed him in the ranks of the Hobey Hat Trick—handled it beautifully, redirecting the puck between his own legs and into the net.

That set the stage for one of the season's defining moments for John McCarthy. By now, McCarthy had proven he could be much more than a great penalty killer and defensive forward.

With the season on the line, though, he returned to the role that initially helped him earn a regular place in the team's lineup. With Vermont pressing to tie the game within a minute of BU taking the lead, he took an absolute beating by getting hit repeatedly with shots. Josh Burrows crushed a slapshot from the left point, and McCarthy blocked it with his right leg. Despite incredible pain, he refused to go down... and ended up blocking a *second* shot by Burrows from the point within ten seconds before barely making it to the bench under his own power once the puck was out of harm's way. It was a great Burn-The-Boats moment: Sacrifice everything because giving in is just not an option.

"McCarthy was already hobbling when he blocked the shot, but the shot bounced back to the guy," Parker recalls, marveling at the effort. "His job was to come back and take away the passing lane, and even though he was in excruciating pain for a while he came back and made sure he covered that passing lane. And then it came back to his point, and he turned around to block the shot and got hit *again*. He still got up—doubly hurt now—and cleared the puck. If you saw how difficult it was for him to get off the ice to the bench, you'd know how hurt he was."

Thanks in part to such heroics, Millan wasn't tested till a power play at 15:02, when Brian Rolloff raced in, only to be denied by the freshman. The Catamounts threatened again at 16:05 on a Dan Lawson shot. For the third time in playoff games over the last two seasons, it was Colby Cohen clearing the puck off the goal line to avert a dangerous chance, batting the puck out of harm's way.

After that close call, the Terriers bounced right back when Wilson nudged a backhanded pass to set up an excellent give-and-go between Lawrence and Higgins. Predictably, Higgins opted to pass while Lawrence finished, firing a high shot beyond Madore's extended glove to make it 2-0 at 16:27. Just 24 seconds later, Wilson almost made it yet another two goals in less than a minute, but Vermont hung tough under pressure.

Then Corey Carlson countered for Vermont with a backhanded shot from behind the goal line at 18:00, attempting to bank it off of Millan and in. Killing a penalty in the period's last minute, McCarthy deflected yet another shot. The co-captain quietly was having one of his best defensive nights of the year. That rounded out the action of a feverish first period with BU owning a 14-7 shot margin and a similar ratio of scoring opportunities.

Early in the second period, it was more of the same for BU. In the first three and a half minutes, it was all Terriers. Like they had during much of the season, the Terriers could smell blood and were going in for the kill. Chris Connolly set up Warsofsky at the two-minute mark, followed by a Nick Bonino shot at 2:45. On that same shift, Bonino rifled a shot from the left-wing circle that squarely hit the crossbar.

Vermont had sometimes struggled to score goals over the course of the season. My sense was that one more Terrier goal might just about end it—even this early. "If we had scored three, that would've been the ballgame," Parker agrees.

With the Catamounts hanging on by their tips of their

claws over a season-ending abyss, everything changed suddenly and dramatically.

Just a half-minute after Bonino rang one off the pipe, Wahsontiio Stacey beat Millan with a shot from the top of the right-wing circle. Suddenly, the momentum swung completely toward the boys from Burlington. At 4:44, BU dodged trouble after a dangerous scramble in the slot looked worrisome. With Vermont pressing hard, BU responded by taking two penalties.

They got through one penalty kill, only to have Vermont get the equalizer at 9:04. The Terriers simply yielded way too many chances. Millan absolutely robbed Colin Vock, but finally Justin Milo knocked it in after the puck bounced to him low in the right-wing circle.

The real stunner came when Vermont gave BU a dose of its own usual prescription by scoring yet again just 42 seconds after the second goal. You could count one hand—maybe even just a few fingers—how many bad goals Millan surrendered all year, but this was one of them. Just after McCarthy was denied on a two-on-one break, Vermont's Josh Burrows took an innocuous-looking shot from the left wing, and it simply eluded Millan. The freshman appeared to be visibly frustrated for the first time that night.

"In goaltending, we talk about a mental reset button," Mike Geragosian says. "In mental preparation, that is so important after you let a goal in. If you let a goal in, let it go. That's so important, especially after a goal that you'd like to have back. You hit a mental reset button. 'Okay, I should have done this, but let it go.'"

Of course, that's easier said than done. In truth, this game proved to be somewhat of a flashback for Millan. He told me weeks later that it was only the second time all season that he had experienced nerves during a game. The first had been the Beanpot opener. Like that game, this Frozen Four appearance was his first on an extremely big venue for even higher stakes.

"It's such a huge stage, and it's something I've never done before," Millan says. "I knew I didn't play well. I just wasn't mentally in the game. I was worrying about what other people were thinking instead of just worrying about stopping pucks. Those games I was nervous because I was thinking about what could happen. I only did that in two of my 37 games this year, but I'd be pretty upset if it cost us."

Curiously he had been quite relaxed up in Manchester, and he frankly placed his jumpy teammates on his back against UNH. No one was more individually responsible than Kieran Millan for the fact that his team had made it to the Frozen Four again at long last. Now, though, his teammates would have to carry him to some degree.

"The problem with Kieran is that when he had an average game, everyone thought he struggled," Mike Geragosian says. "With Vermont, everyone talks about how bad he played. One of those three goals was a wrist shot by a kid with a broken hand. The poor kid caught it and dumped it out to Wilson. It should've been caught and put away. So sticking up for my goalie, he took a little tough rap because of playing so well [for so much of the season]."

"They really took it to us in the second period," Higgins says. "We were all in shock. They scored those three quick goals, and we were thinking, 'This can't be happening. After all our hard work, we're not going to let this happen.'"

Parker called a timeout to regroup. "We were playing well for the most part, other than that spurt," Mike Bavis recalls. "I think [Jack] just wanted to say, 'Settle down here. Let's just get back to the little things and not panic here.' So that was just to have a breather and to hear his voice—calm. When you believe in your team and can convey that 'We're okay, fellas...' I think that's what he was trying to do."

After the timeout, BU's veterans seemed to take it up a

notch. For the rest of the period, the advantage swung back to the Terriers. Colby Cohen hit the inside of a post at 12:15. Less than a minute later, Chris Higgins set up Lawrence again for another terrific chance, then linemate Wilson almost scored on that rebound.

No one wanted to go into the third period down a goal. Fortunately, Trivino got tripped by Patrick Cullity to set up a Terrier power play at 17:06. With just 1:21 left in the second period, Brandon Yip made a great play crossing the puck from the left point to Nick Bonino in the right-wing circle. Bonino slipped the puck through one defender's legs before passing through another to hit freshman Vinny Saponari at the far post for a high one-timer to bring BU back to a 3-3 deadlock.

"I think one of the biggest goals of the year was Vinny Saponari's goal in the second period," Parker says. "We had played great in the first period and were looking pretty good. All of a sudden they're leading and we're second-guessing ourselves. If we'd gone into that dressing room down 3-2 instead of tied 3-3, it would have been really tough. That was an unbelievable play by Yip and a really unbelievable play by Bonino to get it by that guy. So now we go into the third period tied."

"I felt that we were in a good place," Mike Bavis remembers of that point in time. "When you make plays like that, you know your kids aren't tight."

Still, Gilroy was by no means satisfied at that point. "We got outplayed in the second period, bad. We got back in the locker room and said, 'There's no way that Vermont is going to go on to the national championship and we're going to watch that happen.' It was frustrating because we couldn't get anything going."

After the seniors said their piece between periods, BU went right back after Vermont in the third. Brandon Yip had a good chance at 1:20 that seemed to hit a post. The two nearly exiled teammates got together for a chance at 2:45, when Steve Smolinsky hit Zach Cohen with a terrific pass that could not be converted in the crease.

Unfortunately for the scarlet and white, though, Brandon Yip added to his team record for penalty minutes with a cross-check at 8:06. Vermont managed to put home an excruciating power-play goal before the penalty ended. Catamount freshman defenseman Drew MacKenzie—who had not scored a goal during his brief collegiate career— took a shot that went through a screen, caught a few pieces of Millan, and then bled over the line. The goalie again looked uncharacteristically agitated.

The last two times the teams had met, Vermont had broken a 3-3 tie with a third-period goal and gone on to win 4-3. The situation had now been replicated yet again. To paraphrase former Red Sox pitcher Pedro Martinez, you would have to say that if Vermont did this to BU a third time, then the Terriers might have to say that the Catamounts were their daddy.

However, the players remembered the sting of those losses and became fiendishly determined to ensure that good things were not going to come in threes for Vermont. "I felt that way, too," Parker says. "I really felt that we were going to win that game even when they went up 4-3. I thought, 'This game is not going to end like this.' There was no sense of panic on our side."

Just after failing to capitalize on a power play, Jason Lawrence drew two defenders to him before dishing to Higgins. Always preferring to set the table, Higgins attempted to return the pass to Lawrence crashing the far post. Instead, it went off the hand of MacKenzie—who had just scored the biggest goal of his life, not five minutes before—and into the net.

It wasn't purely luck. "Down 4-3, Lawrence makes a quick transition play," Mike Bavis remembers. "Instead of trying to drive wide, he makes a quick cut and he and Higgins run a quick two-on-one. Now did it go off the kid's body and go into the net? Of course it did. But he made a poised play on the attack."

Just over a minute later, Wilson won an offensive-end faceoff to Higgins, who whipped a shot off of Madore's pads. No defender marked Wilson after he won the draw, and he easily potted the rebound on Madore's stick side to make it 5-4. After struggling because of the hand injury suffered against Northeastern a few months ago, there was no question that Higgins finally looked 100 percent healthy. "Once they scored, that just lit us up," Gilroy says. "We just took over that game. That [Wilson, Higgins, Lawrence] line had been struggling offensively down the stretch. They had been working hard but had been snakebitten. To see them take over that game was uplifting for the team—to see them get rewarded for their hard work—that was great to see."

From there on, BU's defensive play was iron-clad. As Bernie Corbett recalls, it was as if the team had sensed that Millan was not quite his usual self, and they made a heroic effort to keep the puck away from the net altogether. It was truly inspiring and the perfect way to repay the debt that they still owed their goalie for Manchester. Once BU secured the lead, Vermont only had one shot on goal and could not get a remote whiff of a scoring opportunity. Finally, the clock ran out, and BU was on its way to the national championship game.

After the game, Terrier alumnus Chris Drury—another member of the 1995 national championship team—sent a text message to associate head coach David Quinn. Chris Higgins remembers it making quite an impact. "Drury said, 'Keep your team away from family and friends who are going to tell you congratulations; this is great. It's only halfway done—they can congratulate you after you win it on Saturday night.'

"That stuck with us and the coaches, and when we got back to the hotel we just said a quick 'hi' to our parents, had our dinner, then went back to our rooms—stayed tight as a team and didn't let any distractions get in our way."

Interviewed on TV for ESPN2, Colin Wilson was asked his thoughts about facing Miami for the title. "I'm sure it'll be a real nailbiter again," Wilson said.

It would turn out to be a game that would lead Terrier fans to bite all ten fingernails and consider starting on their toes.

HITTING THE BREAKS

With focus intact, the team practiced Friday. While most of the team felt good, goalie coach Mike Geragosian recognized that he had some work to do to ensure that Kieran Millan's psyche would rebound very quickly after a game in which he failed to meet his own expectations. Parker likes to joke about Geragosian's role: "When we win, I take credit. When we lose, it's my goalie coach's fault."

After the Vermont game, as the team boarded the bus to go back to the hotel, Geragosian saw Bernie Corbett and quipped, "I don't know whether Jack's going to want me on the bus or under the bus."

Compared to the Beanpot, the challenge was dramatically more difficult for Geragosian. "Not only did he get bombarded, he should've had one or two of those goals back, and Barry Melrose was all over him, like, 'BU won't win with this kid' and 'What did I tell you?' A guy who's not half as knowledgeable as you about college hockey."

Geragosian decided that making practice fun for Millan on Friday would be the recipe to get him cooking again. "Friday was kind of a fun day," Geragosian says. "When we practiced, I said, 'Okay, you lost your twitch a little, we're just going to play aggressive goaltending, and we're going to have some fun.' So we ended it with me putting a bunch of pucks at the blue line, and I had him coming out 15, 20 feet—Gerry Cheevers style—and making these big dramatic saves.

"The last one—I'll never forget this—it went over his

shoulder, hit the crossbar, and went wide. The whole team's watching this, and he just fell down on the ice, laughing and laughing. The whole team was laughing. My Happy Gilmore shot went over his shoulder, hits the crossbar, goes down. I said, 'That's what we're going to do tomorrow—have some fun.'"

Geragosian believes that the Regionals had taken a mental toll on the young netminder, though more after the fact. "He kept complaining about how tired he was. I don't think it even was confidence: He just got mentally drained from the weekend before at 19 years old, you know? He wasn't sleeping... It's a big thing for a rookie."

After that quick practice, there was an autograph signing, meetings, and the always entertaining skills competition. However, the big event for the Terriers was the presentation of the Hobey Baker Award, happening right on the ice surface at the Verizon Center. With Colin Wilson and Matt Gilroy both up for the award and the whole team able to watch from the stands, it proved to be a great way to forget about the fact that the biggest game of the players' lives was just about 24 hours away. "I think that helped a lot," Higgins says. "We were all there to support Matty and Colin. It was good to get distracted and not get us too jacked up."

The program, telecast on ESPNU, was extremely well done. The players' parents were all there—except for Colin Wilson's dad, who had to stay home in Manitoba to keep a close eye on the rising Red River waters that threatened the family property. All of the parents seemed relaxed and were quite amusing, not showing any pre-announcement jitters in the least. Colin's mom reminisced about her days of playing goalie in her kitchen as her son took shots on her for hours, way back in his toddlerhood. "I was a good goalie," she said.

I opted to sit up in the stands. I believed Gilroy would win, but the team and Parker clearly had no clue whatsoever. I wondered if the nominees had any idea or

155

if the presence of the BU band in the arena might provide us all with a hint.

Finally, we learned that Matt Gilroy's improbable ascent from walk-on freshman to coveted professional prospect culminated in being named as Boston University's second all-time Hobey Baker Award winner. After thanking his teammates and coaches, Gilroy saved his last praise for his large family, noting that they were his toughest critics and biggest fans. Any sour feelings about losing his scholarship as a senior had been replaced in favor of humor, as he happily thanked his family for spending a "boatload of money" on his hockey career.

It obviously was a special and exciting moment for the New York native and his family—Gilroy admitted afterwards that none of the three finalists had any idea who was going to win—but it also was a thrill for his fellow seniors. They watched a friend and roommate come a long way from being an unknown commodity compared to some of the big-name recruits in his class. They saw him become an outstanding player on top of turning down over 20 NHL offers to lead the team to a Frozen Four—as well as winning college hockey's biggest individual honor that night.

Immediately after the award ceremony, I chatted with Gilroy's four-year roommates John McCarthy, Steve Smolinsky, and Brandon Yip about it all, as well as checking in with fellow seniors Chris Higgins and Jason Lawrence.

"I'm extremely proud of him," McCarthy said. "Even if he didn't win it, everything he's accomplished this year and over the last four years: It's such a great story that he came in unrecruited. He had to ask to come. It kind of comes full circle now because he's going out on top."

"He deserved it 100 percent," said Smolinsky. "Coach gave him a chance, and just watching him grow over the last four years has been unbelievable. You couldn't ask for a better teammate, a better captain."

With plenty of Terrier fans on hand, as well as the BU band cranking out the tunes during the ESPNU commercial breaks, it was yet another special night in a season of many highs for the program. "It was awesome," Yip said. "Seeing his whole family down there and having the whole team here made it pretty special for him. We're excited to see him bring home the Hobey Baker."

"It's definitely well deserved," Lawrence added. "He's a heck of a player and a better person off the ice than he is on the ice. It's a great award, and he means a lot to this team."

Back in the fall of 2005, it didn't take long for his fellow freshmen to see how much the rookie Gilroy could mean to the team back when he was vying for a place in the Terrier lineup. "As soon as we got to school, we started playing shinny games, and he was one of the best guys on the ice," McCarthy said. "But Coach is always slow with the freshmen, and he took his time getting us into the lineup. Matt got in the lineup four games in and has been there ever since."

"I think we saw it early on freshman year," agreed Higgins. "When he got in the lineup, he stayed in there the whole time and played with Dan Spang, another great player and All-American. He kept getting better and better every year. You could just tell the signs that Matty was going to be a special player and a Hobey Baker candidate."

Smolinsky was Gilroy's defensive partner for several games while Brian Strait was injured. At times, Smolinsky admitted, Gilroy's offensive skills run the risk of turning a teammate into a spectator. "It's fun," Smolinsky said about that experience. "Just watching him get that puck and go is unbelievable. He does pretty much whatever he wants out there. Sometimes you get yourself caught watching him because you never know what he's going to do. He's a special player and an even greater guy."

This was the year we all learned just how great a guy

Gilroy is off the ice. As we have seen earlier in this book, the Terriers' uncharacteristically average campaign the previous season turned out to be a great motivator for Gilroy to return and right the ship as one of its captains. At the risk of mixing metaphors, it's amusing to think of him righting the ship by burning the boats.

Coach Jack Parker often said that having Gilroy and McCarthy as co-captains has been like having additional assistant coaches. Gilroy was certainly not afraid of laying down the law, even if it's with his brother, freshman Kevin Gilroy.

"It's part of being the captain," McCarthy said. "You've got to speak up when guys are not doing what they should do or not playing to their potential. He does that very well. I think the guys have a lot of respect for him. When he speaks up, guys listen."

Yet for the seniors, Gilroy's friendship will always mean more than his many honors or even his great job as captain. "He's been such a great leader, but more than that, he's been such a great friend to all of us," Higgins said. "It's been a great four years; it's been a privilege playing with him, and I'm just so happy for him right now."

It was a great night and an honor that only one Terrier, Chris Drury, had experienced before. Just one thing could make these seniors even happier than they were at that moment. On Saturday night, we would see what Matt Gilroy and his classmates might be able to do for an encore.

PREP COURSE

They would be facing the No. 13 seed, Miami University. After Thursday night's win, Jack Parker had joked about how warm it was in Miami, as if he did not know that the school is located in Ohio as opposed to Florida, which is home to the University of Miami.

Despite the joking and disparate seedings, though,

Parker was not about to take the RedHawks lightly. "At no time did I think this was going to be an easy game. I was so happy that it was Miami and not Bemidji because [we might have underestimated Bemidji] and it would have been so much of Goliath versus David.

"The thing that bothered me the most about Miami is that they should've won the national championship the year before. They had the best team in the nation the year before, I thought. They were the best team all year and then they lost a really tough game to BC in the Northeast Regional final. That kept them from going to the Frozen Four. I've seen that an awful lot, where the team you expect to win the national championship doesn't, and then the next year they win it [like BU in '95 or '78 or Michigan State in 2007]."

"They were one of the best teams we saw on tape all year," Jason Lawrence says.

After the pleasant diversion of the Hobey Baker ceremony and the skills competition, the team set its sights for the championship game. As always, everyone had their own way of preparing. "It's our job to make sure that everybody prepares for the game the way they're most comfortable getting ready for the game," Parker says. "But only if that way doesn't interfere with anyone else getting ready for the game. So if you've got a guy who wants to jump around bare-assed in the dressing room ten minutes before the game, laughing his ass off, while someone else is squeezing his stick and trying to get ready to go, that's a distraction."

Parker's appreciation of the variety of ways in which players need to prepare goes all the way back to his playing days as a Terrier in the late 1960s. One of his teammates, Herb Wakabayashi, had a routine of getting fully dressed for the game… and then sitting in his locker stall, nonchalantly reading *The Boston Globe*. Parker's coach—the legendary Jack Kelley—was a fire-and-brimstone motivator who did not care one bit for

Wakabayashi's routine. Yet what he could say when the forward went out and had his usual multi-point game?

Parker himself is more predisposed to superstition and ritual—less so in recent years, he says, however—though it's important to differentiate between the two. Superstitions exist only to make a player or coach feel comfortable, and no one could argue that they would have an impact on the game. In Parker's case, he shuns white-board markers of his opponent's color. So there is no way he would use, say, a black marker against Providence College. He wears the same game shoes regularly. "They're from the Stone Age," Jason Lawrence says.

After Thursday's win, Agganis Arena rink manager Joe Conceicao and Zamboni driver Mike Cunniff happened to tell Parker about an odd fact regarding the win over Vermont. They had watched the Vermont win from the runway near the Terrier bench. Meanwhile, BU sports information director Brian Kelley spent the game going back and forth between the press box and the ice level near the BU locker room. Conceicao and Cunniff noticed that the Catamounts scored all four of their goals while Kelley was up in the press box.

As a result, Parker told Kelley to make sure he spent the *whole* game down at ice level on Saturday night.

In contrast to superstitions, rituals can be thought of as extremely helpful ways for a player or coach to get in the right mindset for a game. Parker routinely lies down for a while before a game to visualize various situations as he wants them to occur. Some players will envision themselves making a key save or great pass. Others will zone out with headphones on, playing music to rev them up or calm them down.

With Kieran Millan, goalie coach Mike Geragosian kept working hard to ensure that his protégé's state of mind was right where he wanted it to be. "I said 'Positive, sunshine, and I really want you to stay with what we talked about. Be aggressive,'" Geragosian says. "So if you saw one time when he went running out to the corner early and they hit the post, blame me. I pretty much asked Kieran to be a little more competitive and aggressive and to do things more with angles more than range or reaction saves. I definitely asked him to be aggressive and was really proud that he was."

In the minutes before the teams took the ice for the championship game, Nick Bonino sat on the Terrier bench while Luke Popko loitered nearby, both wearing the usual "Burn The Boats" undershirts. Bonino focused on building a sculpture of sorts out of pucks. "I'm an antsy guy; I can't sit still," Bonino says. "I really have no superstition; I just hate sitting around. Before a game, I'll stretch out, and me and Pops will sit out there and shoot the breeze. We're not the kind of kids who sit there with headphones on or with their heads between their knees. We keep it light. Last year I saw the pucks and started making a display. The best is when a guy on the other team across the way starts making a design and we kind of battle it out. I think I'm undefeated on those. In D.C., they gave me 40 pucks, so I was able to make a pretty grand structure."

Bonino's lattice-like structure had supporting columns of pucks stacked on each side, holding up an elaborately connected set of a few dozen pucks on end. It was a modest bit of civil engineering but a useful pregame distraction.

Inside the locker room, a fan who imagined the team solemnly preparing for the biggest game of their lives would have been very surprised at the scene in the dressing room. Several of the forwards were actually dancing. This was not unusual. For most of the season, the defenseman were elsewhere while this was going on, so Matt Gilroy was taken aback when he first learned of this pregame ritual up in Manchester.

"Gilroy got mad at me and Yip once because we were dancing before a game at UNH before the Regionals,"

Colin Wilson remembers. "Normally it's just the forwards; the defensemen are in another room. We were like 'Gilroy, don't worry—we do this all the time.' It's just our laid-back atmosphere. It probably wouldn't have happened if we weren't winning so much."

So it was just business-casual-as-usual for the Terriers before the title game. "Everybody was just doing what they normally do," Wilson says. "I'm out of the dressing room most of the time. The only time I'm in the dressing room is to put on music." As usual, Wilson played his usual array of techno, and the usual group of forwards skanked to it. Definitely one of the more unique pre-game rituals that I've encountered.

Neither Parker nor Bavis were aware of the dancing when I told them about it months later. "I'm glad I didn't know," Parker says.

"Techno?!" Bavis exclaims. Told that Wilson was behind it, Bavis laughs. "Willie, who knows? He did kind of go to the beat of a different drum."

A different drum machine, more accurately.

Eventually the time came for the coaches to address the team before taking the ice. "Jack is fabulous," Geragosian says. "He lets me take the role I want and respects me as a goalie coach. He gives me free rein in scouting other teams. He'll talk to the team and about ten minutes before we go on, I'll talk about the opposing goaltender and most of all the other team's tendencies."

So Geragosian stood up for his usual time slot before the championship game. "I thought the story before the Miami game was very interesting," he says. "I went in there very serious for a change, and I wrote on the board 'If your mind can conceive, your heart can believe. You can achieve.' Now usually I come in and do something fun and just loosen them up, and then Jack comes in and gets them going. It's a setup but a natural setup."

With his earnest words, Geragosian actually struck the wrong note, and he realized it immediately. "Well, I say that, and the whole team's eyes go down. Wow, this isn't the response that I wanted—a downer, like we've gotta really *do* this. So I turned it around and said, 'Okay, here's the deal.' We had a saying all year: We don't toss pucks at goalies; we toss lettuce. 'So remember we don't toss pucks at goalies, we toss?' 'Lettuce!' the players shouted. 'Lettuce! Lettuce! Lettuce!' They're all yelling it, and I leave the room. Jack is leaning on the wall, looking like 'Oh my God!'

"Then Jack came in for the pep talk, and I said, 'See you after the game with the hardware.'"

Another bit of levity arose as the team took the ice. According to Mike Bavis, Bob Richardson—one of the original proponents of the Burn The Boats theme—came up with another idea for this stage of the game. There would be no more speeches from famous ex-Terriers—it would all be about the players in that locker room. The coaches asked the players to take a marker and write 'BTB' on their palms along with the uniform number of the player next to them in the locker room. Sharpie markers were left on the team lunch tables to reinforce the idea.

Bavis himself not only wrote BTB on his palm; he also wrote the three captains' numbers on his thumb, then the seniors' numbers on his fingertips... and finally ALL of the other players' numbers on his hand. 'You're crazy,' Parker told him when he saw his assistant coach's hand, which was almost entirely covered with marker. But when Bavis held up his hand with the numbers on it as the players took the ice, it was a nice way to dispel any tension.

If it was a lighter moment, the theme of Burning The Boats still resonated strongly that night. Colby Cohen remembers thinking about it as the teams prepared to face off. "We're going to win the battle, and then we're going to take Miami's boats home."

A GAME FOR THE AGES

It would be far from easy. Miami came out in the first period and made several immediate statements with physical play. Time and again, a RedHawk player leveled a Terrier with a bone-crushing but clean hit. In fact, the action provided one of the best examples I've ever seen of a college team playing an extremely physical game while also showing extraordinary discipline.

By the end of the night, the penalty totals were lopsided—Miami had seven power plays while BU had just two—but the referees did a fantastic job of calling the game fairly. That's especially impressive when a championship game might make some officials more inclined to have power plays balance out, fairly or not.

"I expected it to be a battle," Gilroy recalls. "I didn't know much about them—who they beat or who they played—usually I just like to go out and play. But after I heard that they swept Michigan and Notre Dame, I just said, 'Oh geez.' Coming in, I knew it was going to be a tough game, and then they just started to run kids. And I said, 'We're in a game.' They came out real physical. There was a lot of hitting and intensity and not a lot of power plays for us. Power plays really get us going, so that was frustrating—that they weren't drawing penalties and they were pounding us."

On one of his first shifts, a RedHawk forechecker buried Corey Trivino in his own zone, and the freshman went off for stitches in his face. Popko took his place on the third line, though the necessity of killing the first two penalties of the game made the forward shortage somewhat moot for the time.

Despite Miami's decisive advantage in terms of hits and power play, though, BU looked like it was going to be okay. Colin Wilson set up Chris Higgins for a chance at 1:20, followed up by Lawrence for another bid. Breaking in over the blue line, Bonino slipped a slick pass to Yip for a shot at 8:07.

Then, seconds later, Wilson won a faceoff to set up another Lawrence shot. BU had several pretty good chances through the first 15 minutes, while Miami didn't get many whiffs of the net at all. The RedHawks had strong puck possession on an early power play, but the majority of the shots were blocked before they reached the net. The Terrier penalty killers did a great job on a second Miami power play, where the RedHawks couldn't get anything going.

Millan looked back to normal when he had some minor tests, and BU continued to get some pretty good chances. Bonino set up Yip again at the 12-minute mark, but the Terriers didn't take the lead until 15:15. The freshmen did the heavy lifting. After receiving a pass from right point to left from Eric Gryba, defensive partner David Warsofsky threw the puck into the slot, where it caromed off of Miami defender Alden Hirschfeld. Miami goalie Cody Reichard couldn't cover the redirected puck, and Chris Connolly poked it in near the far post. It had to be discouraging for Miami given how nicely they had set the physical tone in the game.

After BU killed yet another power play, Wilson set up Higgins for another chance with 1:45 left in the period, and the Terriers mounted their most consistent pressure thus far. Miami finally took a penalty with 13 seconds left before intermission. There was a long way to go, but there was no cause for alarm among the Terrier faithful.

Early on, the second period looked promising, too. On their first power play, BU looked great in setting up plays. A few good shots were muffed, but then Higgins had a pair of great opportunities, most notably redirecting a Colby Cohen shot-pass from the right point that Reichard needed to stop.

But just when things were looking up for BU, Miami tied the game. You couldn't fault Millan at all. On the heels of killing that penalty, Miami suddenly jacked up the pressure. Set up at the right point, Garry Steffes took the initial shot, and the RedHawks were unstoppable on the rebounds. Jarod Palmer took a whack at it and then Andy Miele before Steffes finally reached the crease and buried his own rebound.

It was a little ominous for the Terriers, as it's never a good sign when the defense fails to clear two rebounds and allows a third shot. Sure enough, Miami ratcheted up their intensity and very nearly took the lead. Following his goalie coach's advice, Millan aggressively challenged Justin Mercier by coming out the net, and the talented forward fired a shot from a sharp angle low in the right-wing face-off circle, clanging the puck off the far post. Seconds later, Brandon Yip returned to his home away from home in the penalty box, and the momentum clearly had shifted dramatically in Miami's favor.

Curiously, though, the RedHawks could do nothing with the man advantage, and both teams struggled to get any good shots for the next several minutes, some of which included an ineffectual BU power play. Eventually, it would be Miami to mount an attack again. On a two-on-one break at 9:20, Tommy Wingels shot it just wide.

Ninety seconds later, Miami had an amazing chance when they counterattacked off a BU rush. It looked to be a three-on-one, but Pat Cannone did a clever job of quasi-obstructing Gilroy without getting called for a penalty as the Hobey Baker winner desperately tried to get back to cover. The upshot was a two-on-*none* break! Trent Vogelhuber passed it to Mercier for the last-second shot, but Millan made the crucial save to preserve the tie. It was obvious that the freshman goaltender was back on his game when it mattered most.

BU countered with a rush almost immediately, as Jason Lawrence raced in on the left wing for an excellent backhand move before flipping a shot just wide. The teams had begun to resemble heavyweights exchanging blows.

At 14:15, the momentum was back with the Terriers.

Bonino set up Colby Cohen for a left-point slapshot that hit the near post, and the Bonino-Yip-McCarthy line pressured the net for the rest of their shift. The Wilson-Higgins-Lawrence line followed suit seconds later, with Lawrence stealing the puck and firing a slapshot that Reichard squeezed.

The pendulum proceeded to swing back to Miami. Justin Vaive had a good shot from tight quarters at 16:50, and then a Colby Cohen penalty led to a point-blank power-play shot seconds after that. Once again, Justin Mercier showed what a threat he could be on the attack. He not only drew the penalty—he got off a great shot from close range on the ensuing faceoff, hitting Millan in the mask. Miami's power play was its best since early in the game, but BU continued to hold the RedHawks off. The game would go into the third period knotted at 1-1.

Jack Parker marvels at how well Miami played through most of the evening. "As the game progressed, I was amazed at how hard they played against us, but I was more amazed at how physical they played. They bumped us pretty good and took a lot of our guys out of the game—not that we shied away from it, but they played such a good physical game that they negated a lot of things we like to do.

"They also did a great job at center ice throughout the game. They kept changing up their forechecks, and we knew that they were going to play like Vermont or UMass does sometimes. We had a much easier time getting through center ice two nights before. The thing that really amazed me was I thought that if we could get the puck down low that we could dominate them down low, and we didn't. So I was really impressed with them before we played them, and I was more impressed as the game went on."

During the intermission, the seniors once again asked the coaches to leave the motivation to them. Gilroy remembers it well. "Going into the third period, I said,

'Coach, do *not* come in here. This is us.' We shut the door, and they came in a little later, right before we went out. I think guys liked it, too: It was just our team. It was all about us. Looking back, I think guys will remember those moments when we shut the door and it was just us. It was no more X's and O's. It was just emotional—just get it done.

"We're just reminding guys of what we've been through—that there's no better team than us. We've done this together; we play for each other. We're all in it together, and we'll regret it if we go out any differently. Everyone talks a lot about the leadership this year, but it was so easy. We had to yell maybe a handful of times— yell at the whole team to wake up—but it was such a special group to work with."

"I think they earned that trust," Parker said of his seniors' desire to take the reins from the coaches at critical times—not something that was at all unprecedented in Parker's coaching career. When he did address the team, Parker kept it simple. "We went in and said, 'Do you want to win the national championship? You've got to win the third period.'"

As it turned out, the Terriers would require an extraordinary sequence of events to merely *tie* the third period and send the game to overtime.

That would be surprising. I intuited that BU eventually would bust loose with two or three goals and win it going away. Likewise, Kieran Millan had a sense of inevitability. "Going into the third, it's tied 1-1, and I'm confident," Millan says. "Our record when we were tied or up going into the third period had to be near-perfect all year." That's correct. BU was 25-0-0 when leading going into the third, and 7-1-3 when tied after two periods of play.

So it was startling to see Miami come out and play with even greater intensity in the third period. Yet again, Justin Mercier dazzled the crowd, making a great puck-dragging move to get around Colby Cohen to get off a backhand shot that Millan stopped at 1:20 of the third period.

I kept waiting for BU to step on the gas pedal, but the Miami defense now resembled an immovable object facing a force that was frankly resistible. The shot totals for both teams crept up at pace of about one every two minutes, as the next goal loomed larger all the time.

While BU failed to muster a single grade 'A' chance during the period's first 16 minutes, Miami continued to play hard and bide its time until an opportunity presented itself. When it did, the RedHawks capitalized. At 12:31, Carter Camper deftly stickhandled through traffic in the BU zone before releasing a shot. Millan made the save, but it went right onto the stick of Tommy Wingels for an easy rebound goal.

Still, there was no sense of panic from the confident—even cocky—Terriers. "In the third period, they scored first, and I said, 'Oh, boy,'" Gilroy remembers. "I wasn't worried after the first goal. I just thought, 'Well, this is just going to be more dramatic; we've come back so many times down the stretch.'"

Jason Lawrence got called for slashing just about a minute later, and worries crept in with time running down. The real shock came at 15:52. Just after exhaling when they had successfully finished their seventh penalty kill of the night, BU proceeded to go down by two goals.

Shattenkirk missed an opportunity to get the puck out of the Terrier zone, and Brian Kaufman picked it up around the left point before quickly dishing to freshman Trent Vogelhuber. Skating across the zone as Colby Cohen attempted to mark him, Vogelhuber—one of five Ohio natives on the RedHawks—fired a shot around the defenseman. It managed to catch a corner of the net low on Millan's glove side. Amazingly, Vogelhuber had just scored only his second collegiate goal, and it looked like it could turn out to be the biggest one in Miami history.

Rarely showing emotion on the ice all season between

the pipes, Millan visibly sagged as the RedHawks celebrated a goal that looked likely to clinch the school's first-ever national championship in any sport. "When they scored the third goal, that was the first time I really thought 'Oh my, we might lose this game,' Millan says. "I couldn't believe it went in, and you assume that it's the nail in the coffin. It wasn't a bad goal, but at the same time you feel that those are the kind of saves you've got to make to win a championship. You kind of just feel helpless at that point: We've got to score two goals, and I can't do anything about it."

On the BU bench, there was a sense of disbelief. For a whole season, the theme of Burning The Boats had morphed into a perception that failure was an unthinkable outcome. Now the team had to face falling short as a highly plausible result. "You look at the bench, and everyone had the 100-mile stare," Bonino says. "Everyone was just zoned out and staring straight ahead. It was tough. You look at it and you think, 'How could this happen?'"

"3-1, I remember going to the bench, kind of in shock," Lawrence recalls. "I remember looking over at Chris and thinking, 'Higgs, this is really the way we're going to go out? We're not going to win this thing.' I can't remember if I just *thought* that or said it. But then I remembered that we had scored goals pretty fast against BC. I figured we'll see what happens."

"I mean, there's nothing else you can do but believe," says McCarthy. "We didn't want to think that we're going to lose. You just had to have the attitude of 'let's get one; let's chip away at it.' That's the only thing you can do. There's no option."

"When they scored again, the sails deflated," Gilroy says. "I remember thinking, 'I can't believe that this is how it's going to end.' I remember on the bench trying to say stuff like, 'C'mon, let's go!' and then thinking that I sounded like an idiot. Then the coaches started saying it."

Improbably to him, Gilroy's exhortations seemed to catch on, fanning a small spark to make one final stand. Yet there was also a big decision to make. When should Millan be pulled from the net in favor of an extra attacker? Immediately after the third goal was scored, David Quinn had walked over to Parker. "I went down to Jack and said, 'The next offensive-zone faceoff I think we've got to pull him.' He looked at the clock and said, 'There's a lot of time.' I said, 'We're on life support right now. If they score, it's over, but we definitely need to score.' Given the way the game was going, it just felt like the right thing to do."

Quinn's assertion was no surprise. As a general rule, the assistant coaches tended to have a more aggressive philosophy than Parker when it came to pulling the goalie early. "Quinny and I think earlier, and Coach over the years has seen that fail," Mike Bavis says. "So our automatic instinct is to think early when pulling the goalie. At 2-1, I was already starting to think about six-on-five plays. Coach and I were talking, and I was thinking aggressively. Coach historically thinks that's early, and statistically I think he'd be proven right—if you pull him too early you're going to get scored on."

One major consideration was not just the score and the time remaining but how BU had been playing all period. If they had been buzzing the Miami net—hitting pipes and getting robbed by great goaltending—all three coaches may have felt differently. "If we were down 3-1 but getting some chances, it would've felt too early," Bavis says. "We really didn't have anything going for about 12 minutes. In general, we didn't have much going in the third period. Their trap took us out of our rhythm—really got us overthinking and disrupted our flow—so it felt like 'we've got to do something here.'"

For all of his decades as a coach, this was one of those times when Parker wrestled with an exceptional level of doubt. As Bavis reminded me, assistant coaches make suggestions; head coaches make decisions. Parker flip-flopped on what to do, waffling throughout a two-minute TV timeout that would have given the team plenty of time to make the move.

"During the TV timeout, we talked about it," Parker says. "I just thought it was too much time, in my mind. I'm always of the opinion that you're going to get the second goal before they get the fourth goal. In order to get the second goal, it's hard to keep them from getting the fourth goal if you pull the goalie. You still might be able to get a goal here and then pull the goalie.

"So I had decided we're not going to pull him. I started to send him back out and then I said, 'Well, that's an asinine thing to do.' There were two things: One, we weren't playing well enough. When you pull the goalie, either you have intensity or you don't. Most of the time when you pull the goalie, you play at a much higher level of 'gotta get it done, gotta possess the puck, gotta go get it, gotta make sure that nothing goes wrong.' You can change the momentum.

"When you pull the goalie and keep him out, most of the time you're asking your team to play much more focused, much more intense. So that was part of it, and the other argument is, you've got to get two, and there's only three and a half minutes to go here. And the other thing that dawned on me is that I've got two pretty good units that can go every other shift for a while, and I really thought they were going to call a timeout, too. So I changed my mind. Now in order to change to my mind, I've got to call a timeout. So I wasted a timeout."

On the bench, the players actually had mixed feelings, just like their coaches. Chris Higgins was opposed to it. "He pulls the goalie, and us as players were thinking 'What are you doing? We've got plenty of time to score, and one fluke bounce and they make it a three-goal game, and it's over.'"

"I was a little surprised," Millan says. "I had never been

pulled that early down two goals. But we had to score two goals against a team that's really strong defensively, and that's going to take time."

Eric Gryba also recalls thinking it was the right move. "We needed two. The chances of us getting one even-strength with the trap and then getting another one... Obviously, the odds were stacked against as it was, but if we didn't pull the goalies so early, I don't think it would've worked out as it did."

After startling some of his players with the move, the next surprise came with the choice of the extra attacker. As noted earlier, the team had practiced six-on-five play extensively to prepare for the Frozen Four. The top two forward lines were the obvious choice to get all of the play, and Vinny Saponari and Chris Connolly had exclusively practiced to be the sixth man with those two lines.

At the last moment, Parker opted to make one key change. He tapped Zach Cohen—one of the two guys who earned an 11th-hour reprieve from being kicked off the team almost exactly one year earlier. "The ironic thing is that I had never ever put Cohen out there before with those guys," Parker says. "It was absolutely my call; it was a hunch on size. This team has been pushing us around; I think we want Cohen out here with that group.

"Connolly played with the other group; it was Saponari who got sat. When we practice six-on-five, we usually just practice one group. We might even have Wilson and Bonino out there together. You're usually playing for 30 seconds or a minute. So we had practiced that but not with Cohen, and that's what made it bizarro. It was a conscious thought: Cohen's a physical player, and we need somebody in front of the net."

If it was unexpected, it was far from an off-the-wall hunch, as David Quinn told me. "I think he was second on our team in even-strength goals all year even though he was playing eight minutes a game on the fourth line with no power-play time."

"He knows what he's doing," Lawrence says. "Pulling the goalie and putting Zach out there—little tweaks that people don't always see or notice but that always seem to pay off."

No one could have been more surprised than Cohen himself. "He called timeout and pulled the goalie to have six guys out there, and I wasn't expecting to play the last three and a half," Cohen says. "I'd just be a cheerleader for the guys. So Coach told Connolly to go out there with Bonino's line, and right when he was halfway over the boards, Coach goes 'Oh, wait, wait... Conno, come back.' And then he taps me on the shoulder and says get in there. I played one shift, and we got nothing. Connolly went out on the next one, and I was like, 'Do you want me to go again?' And Coach goes, 'Yeah I want you to go again!'"

The early pulling of the goalie led to a few heart-stopping moments—most notably a Miami rush that could have led to an empty-net goal if not for a RedHawk being offside. However, you started to sense that the BU team finally started to elevate its play.

Going way back to the summer—through Mike Boyle's conditioning rigors, the early-morning river runs, the motivational talks from ex-Terriers—a big theme for the season had been raising the bar. Time and again, the team had lived up to that theme, but this would be the greatest challenge of all. Time was tighter and the stakes were the highest that the players had ever encountered in their lives as hockey players.

It's impossible to specify a moment at which BU took control of those last few minutes. You could just sense the intensity and pressure as they mounted steadily. The puck started to linger in the Miami zone for longer periods of time, and the Terriers finally began to dominate the RedHawks down low in the way that Parker believed they would be able to do for much of the game. "I think we got a little more space because they were probably more in a prevent defense," Bavis says. "'Keep them outside, don't get caught overpressuring them.' And it was, 'Wow, we've got some space now.'"

Colin Wilson and Chris Connolly had the first real chances around 1:25, but the puck went into the crowd for a faceoff six seconds later. BU certainly was looking better on the attack, but it looked like it would be academic for the Terrier collegians with just 79 ticks left.

During that short break, David Quinn happened to notice something. "With 1:18 to go, I vividly remember that I turned to my right to look at a faceoff, and out of the corner of my eye I caught Miami's bench, and they were celebrating. They weren't being obnoxious; they weren't being arrogant, but they were celebrating. And I can't blame them. They weren't being disrespectful, but you could see the jubilation in their faces and in their body language."

Around this time, an interesting development arose at a bar in the neighborhood. "I was talking to [concert promoter] Don Law a few weeks ago," Parker told me several weeks later. "He's a big giver to the program and a classmate of mine from BU. He had a lot to do with getting Agganis Arena built—a lot. He was down with his son and a friend who had his grown son with him. After the game was over, Don went back to his hotel room with his son, but his buddy with his older son went to a bar right near the rink.

"When they went in, the entire bar was set up with glasses of champagne, but people hadn't really gotten in there yet. So the guy says to the bartender, 'What's this?' And the bartender says, 'This is unbelievable. Two guys from Miami came in when they went up 3-1 and ordered every single bottle of champagne to be opened and poured and paid for it. They invited everyone over for a champagne toast, and then when BU tied it up 3-3, they just left. They had already paid for the champagne. I've

175

never seen them since.'"

Apparently some premature celebration occurred just down the runway from the Miami bench as well. "I heard that with a couple of minutes left in the game the NCAA brought the trophy down behind Miami's bench," Gryba says. "I guess they brought the trophy to the runway behind the bench—somewhere back there. I guess the scratches—the guys that weren't playing that night—were like holding it, touching it, kissing it. They had it, and then they took it away because the game wasn't over, and we won it. So don't count your chickens before they're hatched."

At least one former Miami player allegedly sent a mass text message to the RedHawk players, wanting to be the first to congratulate them on their great accomplishment.

All of the champagne bubbles would go flat. The trophy would never reappear. It would turn out to be the largest buzzkill in the history of an NCAA championship game in college hockey.

To be fair, though, Enrico Blasi never looked like a coach who had the game won. According to David Quinn, "Someone said that Rico was telling the team 'Don't let up for one second. Don't let your foot off their throat; they can score two goals in a blink of an eye.'"

Within seconds of the ensuing faceoff, BU nearly scored. Bonino won the draw to Yip, who fired a wrist shot through traffic. Somehow Reichard made the save. The puck bounced around, and Yip brought it behind the net.

Cycling the puck, Bonino got it and flipped it on net— perhaps a bit hastily. "Yip made a great drop," Bonino says. "When I look at the film I'm kind of upset with myself. If I'd just lowered my shoulder and gone to the net I would have a lot better scoring chance. It kind of looks like I shy away. I was trying to get it up quick, but the kid got it. If he had pushed it to the corner, it would have been a whole different story, but he held it there and I was able to get it back to Cohen."

That's an understatement. After Bonino's shot, Miami defenseman Cameron Schilling had the puck on his stick to clear it, but Bonino simply stripped the puck from him and nudged it over to Zach Cohen.

"Nick made a great play behind the net to keep the puck right there," Cohen says. "I got a hold of it and just tried to lift it as high as I could. I wasn't looking. You figure anything can happen. My mindset when you're out there six-on-five is you've just got to shoot it, no matter what. I didn't see it go in. I was like 'Where did it go?' And then I saw it bounce in behind him, and Yip jumped up."

Replays showed just how small an opening Cohen managed to find with the blind shot. On the short side of the net, Reichard had left only a gap of several inches from his armpit down to the top of his right leg pad. Cohen's shot appeared to carom off of the goalie's right pad—and maybe off his side—before sneaking in under his armpit.

Still, the Terriers were fortunate that Cohen managed to end up with possession in that situation." The puck never should've got back to Cohen," Parker says. "They flubbed a couple of chances, and that's what makes the difference."

Suddenly, it was a one-goal game. Still, there now were only 59.5 seconds remaining. "When that one went in, it was exciting," Bonino says. "We had a glimmer of hope."

"Finally we get it down there for some time, we're buzzing, and Zach Cohen scores," Gilroy says. "I remember saying to myself, 'Okay, we're going to make a game of this at least.'"

Kieran Millan felt even more optimistic, reflecting on the fact that Miami was a young team with a freshman goalie. "I really did feel as soon as we scored the first goal that we'd tie it up."

A few fans recalled that the team had been undefeated all season whenever Bonino notched at least one point, and he had just done so for the first time in this game. "Some family friend or someone's mom or dad said, 'Well,

we've got a lot better shot now that he's got a point,'"
Bonino says. "You can call it coincidence or whatever, but
it's a cool little stat."

That set the stage for a heart-stopping final minute of
regulation. Again, Bonino recalled his role in starting the
key play by criticizing himself. "The last one, right after I
got out there the puck was against the boards and I made
this spin play. I had a lot more time than I realized, and
I just threw it toward the net. So much was going on—I
was in too much of a hurry."

Hastily thrown at the net with a backhander from the
right-wing boards, the puck was far wide of the net on
the near side. However, it caromed off the back boards
and went right on the stick of Chris Higgins. "You try not
to think too much; you just react," Higgins says. "I got
the puck along the sidewall and made a play to give it to
Gilroy at the center point."

A right-handed shot, Gilroy received the puck on his
forehand, but Mercier was racing over to cover him from
the forehand side, so he quickly slipped the puck onto his
backhand.

"I remember Higgy getting the puck and he saw me
coming down," Gilroy says. I didn't know what was
going on; I just played. Everyone talks about the pass
that I made, but if you look at the play, there was about
27 guys in front of me and Nick Bonino just sitting there
wide open to my right. I saw him out of the corner of my
eye, but if I looked right in front of me there was so much
action and a bunch of guys ready to play goalie."

In the heat of the moment, Gilroy somehow managed
to see Bonino to his right with his stick cocked, ready
to shoot—far to his side and almost behind him—and
feathered a backhanded pass with a remarkably soft touch
across the slot. "I saw that Matt saw me," Bonino says.
"Playing with him all year on the power play, I knew that
this puck was coming to me. He made the move to his
backhand—wasn't really in a great position to shoot, he

178

would have needed to bring it back to his forehand—and made just an unbelievable play. To players like him, it probably is the easiest thing in the world.

"I hit it with everything I had toward the center of the net. I don't remember [if I saw it hitting the net]. I remember Willie at the side of the net, and the place just erupted. I just couldn't believe it."

Bonino's shot barely managed to elude RedHawk defenseman Brad Robbins, who slid attempting to block the shot, as well as the arm of Reichard.

What was going through Bonino's head as he celebrated? "Holy crap, probably."

There were just 17.4 seconds left on the clock. In frustration, Miami defender Matt Tomassoni angrily slashed Jason Lawrence in the back of the legs and was lucky to not get called for a penalty. Gilroy gleefully jumped up on Bonino's back.

On the bench, the ESPN cameras managed to capture the whole BU team leaping up and somehow meshing into a frenetic circle on the tight, long rectangle of the bench. "Once he scored, the best scene of that game is when they go to the bench, and all of the coaches and guys just come together," Gilroy says. "That was one of the coolest things."

"It was just surreal, even to think about it," Zach Cohen says of the tying goal. "I still get goose bumps every time I see it."

"It's a feeling I won't forget all my life," Chris Higgins says. "It was one of the biggest highs of my entire life."

While the tying goal was a display of great talent by several of the team's best players, there was also some luck involved. Parker notes that it might have been a less happy ending if it were not for the fact that Chris Higgins or Matt Gilroy happened to be right-handed shots. "If Higgins had been a left shot, he would have had to go indirect to Warsofsky instead of right to Gilroy. If Gilroy was a left shot, he probably would've shot it, too. He's a

179

right shot, and the defender had the right shot blocked, so the only thing he could've done is shoot a backhander or shoot it off the net for a rebound. He wasn't going to get it to the net, that's for sure."

Millan did not linger on the bench to celebrate. Almost immediately, he jumped over the boards and skated back to his crease. Still, the drama was not quite over in regulation. In the last five seconds, Miami's Vogelhuber looked intent on being an improbable hero yet again. He rushed in with the puck and got off a shot from the right wing. Millan fumbled the puck, and BU fans had their hearts in throats as Pat Cannone swiped at it and missed with one second left before the goalie covered it. "The guy came in and shot it, and I thought that there was less time than there really was," Millan admits. "So I just stopped it, but then I thought I'd better cover it. The guy came in kind of close before I got it covered. It looked scary, but I think it looked worse than it really was. I wasn't worried about it."

The same could not be said for Mike Geragosian. "He was a little tight when he bobbled the puck with a second left. I said to Jack, 'I think I'm going to need this ice-making more than Miami.' I went in there and said, 'Let it go, okay?' It was all short and positive encouragement. I think he needed a coach close to him then. I said, 'We've worked for this all year, and we're going to get it done.'"

Otherwise, the Terrier players, coaches, and staff were in sky-high spirits. "I remember walking down the runway," Gilroy says. "Everyone who wasn't playing that night, our equipment manager [Mike DiMella], everyone was all jacked up—hitting each other, saying 'We got this! We got this!' We get in the locker room and shut the door, and everyone was just 'This is ours.'"

Spirits were a little *too* high in Parker's opinion. He had to remind the team that they had only tied the game and not won it. In 1991, he had seen his team storm back to tie the championship game in dramatic fashion, only to lose in triple overtime. So he knew too well that it could happen again.

Meanwhile, it has to be said that Miami did an amazing job of regrouping during the intermission. "The fact that they didn't lay down and die..." Parker says. "How are you going to get them out of that dressing room after what just happened? They must've gotten so pissed off and just said, 'It's not over yet, boys.'"

"There was definitely still a good amount of confidence," Miami player Brian Kaufman said at the post-game press conference. "We felt it was the same thing going into the third period—tie game, it was going to take one shot to win it."

It was just BU's fifth overtime game all season, and the previous four had ended in ties. While Miami continued to play hard, BU was clearly the better team throughout overtime. At 1:30, Jason Lawrence took a shot while falling to one knee, and Higgins almost buried the rebound while a defender smashed him into Cody Reichard. The goalie's mask flew off during the collision, and the subsequent whistle ended that threat.

Probably playing the game of his life to date, Trent Vogelhuber had another chance in the early going for Miami. Still, BU had the bulk of the opportunities. That doesn't necessarily mean much in overtime, though. Many times I've seen a team dominate in one end, only to have the opposition score on the first chance going the other way. So I wondered if this could end that way, too, as I watched Colin Wilson fight off a check on the right-wing boards after an end-to-end rush to fire a shot right into Reichard.

Two minutes later—after Tommy Wingels and Carter Camper threatened for Miami—John McCarthy had a great chance to be the deserving hero. Yip threaded a pass from the center point for a redirect by McCarthy just aside the crease on Reichard's glove side, but the freshman made the save.

Ultimately, Colby Cohen would score the goal to bring home the team's seventh big prize of the season at 11:47 of overtime. With the freshmen forward line on the ice, Cohen carried the puck out of his own end. Going into the neutral zone, he fired a pass ahead that Corey Trivino redirected into the Miami zone. RedHawk defenseman Kevin Roeder pursued the puck behind the net and seemed to have the advantage in the race for possession, but Trivino hustled after him before going around him to poke the puck loose. Chris Connolly fetched it out of the corner on the left-wing side before sending a backhanded pass to Kevin Shattenkirk at the left point. Utilizing a slick move that he had shown off earlier in the season as well, Shattenkirk stickhandled toward the opposite point, drawing two defenders toward him before dropping a blind pass behind him to his defensive partner. The move gave Cohen a little space, and he skated in before winding up to fire a slapshot.

In front of Reichard, Vinny Saponari skated across the crease with a defender in pursuit, completely screening the netminder. Meanwhile, Kevin Roeder slid onto his side attempting to block the shot. He got a piece of it with his leg, and the puck fluttered through the air quite slowly before it went over the goalie's left shoulder and into the net. Reichard never saw it.

"I saw [Roeder] start to go down, and I was trying to shoot high," Cohen says. "I *did* shoot high: The puck was already on the way up, and it nicked the top of him. It didn't really hit him square. I saw it hit him and float in the air. I know that there were a lot of quotes about me closing my eyes [given that Gilroy had joked about that in the post-game press conference]. I didn't close my eyes—Gilroy was just joking. I saw it hit his leg, and it slowed down. I started to celebrate before it hit the net because I saw where it was going.

"You definitely can't blame the goalie. He had an impressive game, and you can't blame him for the goal."

"Kevin makes a great play, sacrifices his body," Blasi said afterwards. "Goes over Cody's head and into the net. That's what happens in overtime, you know?"

"It was a fortunate goal by big-time players," Parker says. "For Shattenkirk to make a drop pass like that with two guys who could've gone in two-on-oh the other way in overtime of the national championship is something else. He's not always safe, but you don't want to take that away from him.

"Colby Cohen is a real good offensive defenseman because he passes it real well and shoots it real well. He shoots it a ton. But Shattenkirk is a real creative guy, and he made a real creative play there, that's for sure."

Curiously, Colby Cohen celebrated by racing out of the Miami zone and throwing off his gloves around the red line before he was mobbed by his teammates way back in the BU zone. "I knew as soon as I did it that the bench was going to rush me, so I was trying to delay getting dog-piled as long as I could. I thought for sure that I would end up on the bottom of a 25-person dog pile and that it would be pretty painful, but somehow I managed to stay on my feet. Everyone was screaming."

At that point, it quite literally was all over but the shouting. However, the celebration that started right then would continue for weeks to come.

For everyone connected to the program, though, the memories will persist for a lifetime.

FINAL SCORE AT END OF PERIOD THREE:

Boston University Record: 8 Wins 1 Loss (35-6-4 for the season)
Goals: Boston University 34, Opponents 22 (BU 177, Opponents 91 for the season)
Championships: Hockey East tournament, Northeast Regional, National Championship (Seven titles to date for the season)

OVERTIME

The Celebratory Aftermath

ICE PACK

As the players vaulted the boards, flung their gloves skyward, and raced across the ice to collide with Colby Cohen in a jubilant scrum, the coaches joined in a calm embrace behind the Terrier bench. "Somebody said it looked more like relief than excitement, and there's something to be said for that," Mike Bavis says. "It was such an emotional roller coaster to be there... When they got those two goals, you just didn't see it coming as a coach."

Watching the players celebrate, Jack Parker found himself reflecting on the senior leadership. "I was really happy for our seniors, especially our two captains. Johnny McCarthy had kind of a grueling career here, and Matty was going to leave, didn't leave, was it the right decision? Within two nights, he wins the Hobey Baker and wins the national championship and soon to sign a $3 million contract. That worked out right for Matt Gilroy. Then guys like Lawrence and Yip having their best years as seniors, and Higgins was on the verge of having his best year before his injury. Even Smolinsky, getting to play."

On the other end of the ice, it was a sad scene.
Goalie Cody Reichard heaved with sobs in the crease,
surrounded by teammates unable to comfort him.
Blank stares and buried heads were all you could see
on the Miami bench. Eventually the RedHawks pulled
themselves together for the traditional handshake line.

While most of the players were exuberant, Kieran Millan
found himself feeling for the opposing seniors, as usual.
"One of things I really noticed this year, whenever we
knocked a team out, [was that] winning is great, but at the
same time you see those guys who are seniors and might
not play hockey again. Once you've finished shaking
hands, and you're celebrating, you realize that these guys
have just played for four years and probably had been
playing hockey since they were five years old. This has
been their life, and this was their last shot. So you feel a
little bad about taking that away from them."

Meanwhile, I was sprinting downstairs from the press
box, eager to get out on the ice to join the celebration.
When I reached the ground level and dashed around
a corner to a long hallway, I could see team managers
Amanda Gibson and Whitney Delorey along with Hockey
East intern (and former team manager) Elizabeth Paige
Fierman ahead of me. They had taken off their high heels
and were sprinting barefoot. To my surprise, I didn't
make up any ground on them.

By the time I reached the ice, Miami had left the scene
of the crime. Bavis's kids and Parker's grandsons were
out on the ice, and the players pulled together for photos,
scrambling around to dive in front for the shot. The
trophy was presented to Parker, who passed it along to
his co-captains, who turned it over to the seniors. For all
of his antics as class clown, Brandon Yip showed a tender
side when he kissed the trophy.

Colby Cohen collected the trophy for most outstanding
player. It was a great feeling, being out on the ice in this
great arena with the team in a total state of elation. Jason

Lawrence randomly jumped into Colby Cohen's arms and swung around in a circle, as trainer Larry Venis took care to ensure that Lawrence's skates didn't slice anyone in the process. Nick Bonino and Kevin Shattenkirk picked up a vat of Vitamin Water and attempted to sneak up on Parker to give him an impromptu shower. It took a few minutes, but they finally succeeded. Dripping wet, Parker took off his glasses and stood speechless for a minute or two, literally and figuratively soaking it all in.

I heard the healthy scratches comparing notes on the chaos as they all attempted to get out on the ice. "I *totally* took out Ruikka," somebody said. Brian Strait puzzled over whose equipment was whose among the flung gloves and sticks. I thought I probably should interview someone, but I didn't want to interrupt the moment for a good while. Eventually, Parker came over and hugged me, saying, "Thanks for being with us all year... and for all of these years."

Finally I grabbed Eric Gryba for a quick interview, asking him what it felt like to be standing on the ice as a national champion. "It's surreal," Gryba said. "It still hasn't hit that we came back from a two-goal deficit to tie it up and put it in overtime. Then to score in overtime: It's unbelievable. It still hasn't sunk in. This is probably the best experience of my life so far."

CARDIAC KIDS

We headed collectively into the locker room. Brandon Yip fired up Wilson's iPod to play "Championship Pop Bottles" by Lil' Wayne. Between concerns about copyright and gratuitous profanity, I won't cite the lyrics here, but they do allude to winning a championship game. Bonino launched into a goofy sort of hip-hop dance, as Joe Pereira made a big show of polishing the trophy with a towel. A few other players got into the groove until Parker came in and told everyone to quiet down, as BU president Robert Brown was on his way.

Brown gave a very warm and gracious speech to congratulate the players, finishing it by noting that "none of you can go pro next year." That elicited a hearty guffaw from the team.

Next, Parker gave an impassioned speech of congratulations in the locker room. "With our seniors, it's like I had extra coaches all along here... You seniors did it all and did it to the nines. Every game was tough; every game was an unbelievable win except for the Ohio State game. Every game was a tough win in the Hockey East tournament. You guys just kept it up and kept it up and kept it up.

"There has never been a BU team who's won seven titles and six tournaments, ever. You did it all. Anybody in your way, you pushed them aside and you won. You took a little long tonight..."

The players snickered.

"You gave *me* a heart attack. But I'll tell you: It was even better that way, wasn't it? It was even better. Better than winning 4-1. It was an unbelievable game by a whole bunch of people. No sense talking about one guy. It was big-time players making big-time plays all the time, and you guys got it done. I couldn't be more proud of you guys."

Then Parker returned to a theme that he had brought up before the game. "As a player, I never won a national championship. As a player, Mike Eruzione never won a national championship. There are a lot of great players who played here and had great years but never won a national championship. And I'm telling you that every one of those guys was hoping you'd do it, and they feel like they won it with you. Jack Garrity: I hope he's still alive after this game, but I guarantee that he won it with you. Chris Drury, he won it somewhere. Jacques Joubert, the captain of the '95 team, called me from Florida tonight. He won it with you, too. You won it for everybody, boys, but most importantly you won it for the 27 guys in

188

the room. Terrific job, congratulations... and now... it's Saturday night!"

A big whoop arose from the team. The music came back on, and the dancing recommenced. Leaving that scene behind, I walked alongside Bonino and Gilroy down the corridors to the press conference. "That was the sickest game ever," one of them said to the other.

After being around the euphoric teammates, it was instantly sobering to walk into the Miami press conference, which was in progress as we walked in. Blasi said all the right things but understandably seemed a bit stunned. There were a few really long pauses in his answers, as if he were still trying to make sense of it all. Later, I saw him walking slowly down the hall. A few very distraught supporters came up and said how sorry they were, and the coach was the epitome of dignity as he thanked them and moved along.

RENAISSANCE FAIR

The team had been staying at the Renaissance Mayflower Hotel, about halfway between Dupont Circle and the White House. They returned to a total mob scene in the lobby shortly after midnight. "It was unbelievable how many people were there in BU gear," Yip says. "It was a pretty big lobby with two floors, and it was packed. I couldn't even move."

The scene reminded Parker of a few legendary moments in Boston sports with a Broadway show thrown in as well. "When we got off the bus, getting through the hotel lobby and downstairs to have our meal was surreal. That was fabulous. There was such excitement and such a huge throng. I almost felt like I was Jim Lonborg trying to get off the field [when the Red Sox won the American League pennant] in '67 or Havlicek getting off the court [after stealing an inbounds pass to clinch an Eastern Conference championship in 1965]. I did feel like Eva Peron on top of that balcony: 'Don't cry for me, Argentina.'"

Writing in *The Boston Globe,* columnist Dan Shaughnessy penned one of my favorite lines capturing the scene: "He could've been the Pope on the balcony of St. Peter's Basilica."

Parker told the crowd that it had been the best championship game ever played, and who was about to disagree with him?

Subsequently, Parker came up with a plan. It turned out to be his first tactical move of the day that ultimately failed. "I caught up with my wife. She had a glass of wine in her hand, and I said to her, 'I'd like to stay here about half an hour, say hello to everybody we can, and then get out of here. Let's go down to the Mall and take a look at the Lincoln Memorial at night.' She had never seen it at night.

"She said, 'Alright, give me 20 minutes, a half-hour.' So about a half hour goes by, and I go back and say, 'C'mon, let's go.' She said, 'Fifteen more minutes.' I said, 'Okay.' So I came back after 15 minutes, and she's got *two* glasses of wine in her hands. I realize we're not going anywhere now!"

Meanwhile, Matt Gilroy had just reached the pinnacle of his playing career. Given that he wears the number 97 in honor of his brother and how he taps his chest three times before each faceoff in honor of his late brothers and uncle, it occurred to me that winning the national championship might have led him to some especially meaningful reflection on his brother Timmy. For that matter, I figured that all of the media attention might be meaningful to Matt, as it meant that Timmy's story became known to millions for the first time through ESPN and countless news articles nationally.

I should've known better. His connection with his departed love ones is such a fixture in his everyday life— on any day, no matter how action-packed or uneventful— that this was personal business as usual for Matt himself.

"I think it made it a lot more special for my family," he

says. "They don't get to live it like I do because I wear the number every day. But seeing the story all over the place and old friends contacting them and reliving moments about Timmy or Brian—old friends becoming new friends again, old family members coming out of the woodwork and seeing us, all the love that I got down the stretch— that was pretty special.

"But it didn't make me think any different or make me think about Timmy any more or any less. That's always there and I'll always think about it."

Then I ask Matt a more difficult question. Obviously he has drawn a remarkable degree of inspiration from Timmy's memory. Does he believe that he would have ended up being as successful, ironically, if this tragedy had never happened?

Gilroy chews that one over for a good while. "I think I would have been successful quicker if he were still around. Timmy challenged everyone in the house, and he challenged me a lot. I was more athletic than him; I was better put together than him, but Timmy would try to beat me every day. He did not care. He could beat me, and that would make me so mad, and he loved it. If he was still around, the competitive edge of seeing him do better would have made me more competitive quicker. I'd love to have him back, but I've learned so much from him. If he was still around, we might've killed each other maybe, too. We were so competitive with each other."

TERRIERS PART RED SEA

As the team flew back to Boston, athletic director Mike Lynch told Jack Parker that the university had quietly planned a duck boat parade on Commonwealth Avenue to celebrate the championship. Parker didn't exactly embrace the concept. "I said, 'Are you shittin' me? That's a bad idea. Parades are for the Celtics, the Red Sox, the Bruins. They're not for us. A duck boat parade for BU hockey?'"

It turned out to be an amazing experience. "People say you don't appreciate this till a year down the line," Parker says of the whole aftermath. "Well, I don't think it'll ever get any better than it was that week: winning it—the parade was unbelievable. That to me was bizarre. I would've bet the mortgage on my house that we wouldn't have had 15 people around. That was unbelievable, and [Executive Vice President] Joe Mercurio played a big part in that.

"It's a good thing that they didn't ask me beforehand, because I would've said 'No, no, we're not doing that.' But they didn't bother asking me because they knew I wouldn't want to be planning something like that because you've got to plan that weeks in advance. So they were planning it before we went to D.C."

Like Parker, the players viewed the parade with extreme skepticism. Matt Gilroy recalls talking it over with McCarthy, Yip, and Smolinsky as the players ate breakfast at T Anthony's restaurant that morning. "Why are we going to this? No one's even going to be there… Then we got to Marsh Chapel, and it was a mob scene."

It was during my lunch hour, so I hopped on my bicycle and was able to pedal alongside the duck boats as the Terrier band and cheerleaders led a procession from Kenmore Square past hundreds of supporters to Marsh Plaza on Commonwealth Avenue, where a crowd of at least 4,000 awaited their heroes. If the Terrier Nation party started at 10:06 p.m. on Saturday night, it was showing no sign of stopping anytime soon.

When the parade reached Marsh Plaza, the time came for the Terriers to part the red sea, walking through the throng of scarlet-clad fans to walk from the street to a platform in front of Marsh Chapel, where Terrier broadcaster Bernie Corbett, master of ceremonies, sported a scarlet sports jacket. A giant cake iced with "2009 Champions" and topped with a chocolate puck and miniature hockey sticks stood on the center of a curiously long table. The crowd soon understood why such a table had been arranged.

Soon Corbett grabbed the microphone and said, "From 'Burn The Boats' to the duck boats in triumph, I'm pleased to introduce the national champion Boston University Terriers." Wearing their white "third jerseys" as they had in every game since their loss to Maine in game two of the Hockey East quarterfinals, the players were introduced by class, starting with the freshmen. When Saturday night heroes Nick Bonino and Colby Cohen were announced, deafening roars erupted from the crowd.

When the seniors were introduced, they strolled in like the magi bearing gifts. First, it was Steve Smolinsky with the Ice Breaker trophy. Next up was Brandon Yip with the Denver Cup. Jason Lawrence followed with the weightiest team prize, the Beanpot. Then Chris Higgins came forth with the regular-season Hockey East Championship trophy, and co-captain John McCarthy added the Hockey East tournament trophy to the growing collection on that very long table.

Naturally, co-captain and Hobey Baker Award winner Matt Gilroy walked in last to the largest ovation of all, carrying the grand prize—the National Championship trophy.

That set the stage literally and figuratively for numerous tributes. "I'm glad to see you gave so many students the day off from school," quipped Boston Mayor Tom Menino. "Let me just congratulate the BU hockey team on the greatest comeback ever... Jack Parker just wants to keep everybody tense to the end. The guys turned it on; they never quit. So I just want to say congratulations to the team. As mayor of Boston, we declare today to be Boston University Terrier Day in Boston."

BU president Robert Brown spoke next. "National championships are rare. This team reached this pinnacle because of a rare combination of talent—and they have loads of it—dedication that started in the summer and

193

ended in the wee hours of Saturday, and belief—belief in each other, belief in their individual ability, and of the dream that they could accomplish together."

Brown reserved his highest praise for Parker. "Your coaching and mentorship on and off the ice are legendary, and we are privileged to have you in our community," Brown told the coach. "We love you... even when you decide to play without a goaltender longer than most."

After Brown went on to extol the "greatest comeback and greatest team effort I've ever seen" and predicted that a decade from now, "at least 40,000 alumni will claim that they were there at the Verizon Center, and no one will admit that they changed the channel with four minutes left." He praised the "young athletes who refused to yield to what others thought was inevitable."

Mike Lynch spoke next and provided Parker with a surprise announcement, telling the crowd that he had the privilege of informing Parker that he had just been named the winner of the Spencer Penrose Award as National Coach of the Year.

Parker then took the podium and enjoyed another thunderous ovation before being quick to note that he was especially pleased to receive the award given that the more recent trend has been to have the whole coaching staff go to Florida to be recognized for the accomplishment.

In his remarks, Parker noted that "this is the best time to be a coach at Boston University because of Bob Brown's presidency." He went on to reflect on the season. "People keep asking me, 'Is this the best Boston University team of all-time?' And I have to say that no other team won this many trophies and this many tournaments and had the heart-stopping trek through the Hockey East tournament and the NCAA tournament as this club did. They also won more games than any other team.

"I think it's easy for me to say right now that this is the greatest team that I've ever coached at Boston University."

Colin Wilson and Nick Bonino responded by giving each other high fives on the platform.

Parker closed by acknowledging that the Terrier students were the biggest incentive to hold today's celebration. "I had a lot of former teammates down at the tournament," Parker said. "To a man, they were talking about the student section. When we were down 3-1, they couldn't believe how hard and how determined the student section was still cheering and the band was still playing. One of the reasons why we wanted to have this today was because a lot of students couldn't get down to D.C. due to the lack of tickets. So to have all of you here today is a great tribute to our university. I can't tell all you students how much I appreciate your support — especially in the last three minutes of the Miami game."

Terrier co-captains McCarthy and Gilroy spoke a few words of thanks to the fans — Gilroy sounding very hoarse, admitting that he hadn't slept much since Saturday night. Then he proceeded to wish Eric Gryba a happy birthday before cutting the cake to close out the celebration.

Afterward, I asked a few team members to reflect on the celebration. "It was awesome," McCarthy said. "So many fans came out today to support us, which is great because they did it all year long. It all still feels unreal to me."

Mike Bavis agreed. "I said to David Quinn before the overtime, 'I can't believe we're standing here right now,'" Bavis said. "It was kind of a time warp; you couldn't rationalize what happened… Looking back on it on videotape, there were some hell of a plays to make all three of those goals. It was like they were unconscious. They just played. It was unreal. They did some things we haven't done all year on some of those plays. It was awesome."

The event gave Bavis a chance to reflect on how much the amazing win has meant to everyone associated with the program. "There are so many great people involved in this at the university, so to be able to share it with them makes it that much more special," Bavis said. "Sometimes you underestimate how emotional it can be. You see people who have been years with you doing this, and you realize how much it means to everybody."

Speaking of which, the day gave Nick Bonino a chance to fulfill one dream while reliving another. "It was cool," Bonino said of riding in the duck boats. "You see the Red Sox do it and it's something you always dream of doing, so it was great for BU to set it up."

Over two days after scoring what will go down as one of the most legendary goals in college hockey history, Bonino was constantly reliving the experience in his mind. "I just watched the replay here, and it still gave me the chills. I got a great pass and just had to put it in. I'll be thinking about that one for a long time."

The sophomore admitted that the puck went in by a much narrower margin than he realized at the moment. "I didn't think it was that close," Bonino said. "I looked at the replay, and it went under the kid's arm and right by the goalie's glove, so I guess fate just wanted that puck to go in the net. It's a great feeling."

With that, Bonino slipped off the podium, swallowed by the red sea.

BREAKING THE MEMORY BANK

The good times rolled for the next few weeks. On top of the usual celebratory team banquet, the team was honored at a Boston Bruins game against the Montreal Canadiens. After sitting up in the skyboxes, the team was called down to the loge area for recognition between the first and second periods. They received a standing ovation and plentiful congratulations for the rest of the night.

Next up was a trip to Fenway Park, where Jack Parker was given a Red Sox jersey with No. 6 on its back, the same number he had worn as a Terrier player. The Sox had asked Johnny Pesky if it would be okay with him if the jersey were made, given that the team had retired the number in honor of "Mr. Red Sox" back in 2008.

Wearing the jersey, Parker threw out the first pitch with his players around him behind the mound. "That was awesome," Jason Lawrence says. "We went down before the game, got to watch a little of the Yankees' batting practice from the side. They introduced us and put the game highlights up on the Jumbotron. The place was pretty much full by then. To see yourself on the Jumbotron at Fenway Park is something awesome. We watched that and then half-mooned it around Coach as he threw the opening pitch. We all were thinking that he was probably going to throw it in the dirt, but he threw a pretty good pitch. Everyone gave us a wicked round of applause, and it's great to be recognized like that in Boston. It's something I'll remember all my life."

Despite all of the elation, the players still found themselves attempting to process what they had accomplished for weeks afterward. "It's still hard to believe that we actually did that," Gryba says. "It wasn't just winning the national championship; it was coming from two goals behind with a minute to go to do it. I still have to confirm in my mind that that actually happened."

"It probably took a week or a week and a half for it to sink in," Lawrence recalls. "We were so excited. To have a goal set at the beginning of the year and take six months of hard work in the rink on a daily basis... To accomplish that goal at such a high level, it's something where you can't really explain your emotions. To have a team sport and to be able to win it with a group of guys that you've become brothers with over the course of the year, your excitement level is so high."

Steve Smolinsky says that he always will have fond memories of his four years—the Gilroys or his parents cooking for the players, just hanging around with the guys, everything. Of course, the national championship was the icing that made the cake all the sweeter. "It was a perfect ending for everything. I couldn't have been happier; my parents couldn't have been happier. Especially with how my career had gone for the whole four years, to end up playing the last two weeks and play for the national championship was unbelievable."

Best of all, Smolinsky conquered his fear of failure when the stakes were the highest. "Steve Smolinsky might have played the best game of his career against Miami," Mike Bavis says. "He was on the puck and being physical. I couldn't be happier for a kid like him."

"I wouldn't trade it for anything," Smolinsky says. "And I said that before we won the national championship— because of all the guys that I've met here. It was still worth it to me even though I didn't play as much as I might have wanted to. And the way it ended was really special, especially the way we did it."

It's telling that Higgins says that his happiest memory was more the everyday experience of team togetherness. "It's 26 of my best friends that I'll stay in touch with forever. Just coming to the rink every day, knowing I was going to be with my 26 best friends, trying to get better every day. Then just putting the jersey on every Friday and Saturday night, going to battle. That's something I'll never forget."

David Quinn still marvels at the team's knack for coming through in the clutch. "We were so in the moment. We were winning championship after championship and just ho-humming it. We win the Denver Cup and the Beanpot and the Hockey East, and it was like 'Alright, what are we going to win next?' The mindset was unlike anything I've been around. We were never satisfied, which is a unique thing."

While Parker believes that the immediate aftermath was the best it will ever get, Quinn told me when we spoke in mid-May that the magnitude of the team's accomplishments had been dawning on him more recently. "In the last six weeks, the more I start thinking 'Holy Jesus, this was a special season.'

"I remember [UNH Associate Coach] Scotty Borek saying to me, 'To give you some idea of how good you were, we played a perfect game against you in Manchester and still couldn't beat you. I've got to imagine that Miami played as good a game as they could against you, and they couldn't beat you. That gives you an idea of how good your team was.'"

Given that Parker had acknowledged this BU team to be the best in the program's history in his opinion, I can't resist asking him another tough question: Was Bonino's tying goal the biggest goal in the long history of Boston University hockey?

Jack Parker sits back and looks up at the ceiling for a full 32 seconds. I can see him scanning his memory banks and weighing plausible alternatives. Finally he makes eye contact with me again. "I can't think of a bigger one," he says.

"I'm going back to national championship games and Hockey East games or ECAC games. I would say it was the biggest goal because it made a national champion, but it also made a game for the ages. There's a difference between winning the national championship and winning the national championship in a game that everybody will remember forever.

"The thing about winning this tournament was where we won it, the way we won it, and the fact that we were supposed to win it and did. There have been a lot of national champions, but there has never been a national champion that won it the way we won it. You could say Northern Michigan winning it in triple overtime against us, but in order for it to get to overtime *we* were the ones who had to tie the game, late in the game. If we had won that game, it would've been very similar to the Washington game."

Given the improbability of the team's last-minute, heart-stopping comeback in the nation's capital, Bavis has a hard time thinking that it was anything other than fate to account for the outcome. "I tell you that I believe in it. I honestly believe it. Throughout that week in D.C., I don't know if we were destined, but the way it ended… People will say it's luck, and I question that because the plays that we made were pretty high end."

Parker views it differently. "Fate is such an abstract concept. Destiny is an abstract idea. But just as abstract is luck, and I think you've got to be lucky to get through eight games—the Hockey East Championship, the Regionals, and the Frozen Four. Things have got to fall your way or bounce your way. UNH hits a pipe…

"I would say it's a combination of preparation and skill coming together with luck. Is it God-given? Did somebody pray upstairs? Are Meryl Herman and Mark Bavis and Scotty Cashman up there, working their magic? I certainly believe in God, and I believe in the power of God, and I believe in the power of prayer. But Miami must have some people in heaven, too."

You can't talk about the way BU won its big games without thinking about the impact of a stand that a Spanish conquistador took to rally his troops almost a half a millennium ago. There is no question that the team managed to walk the talk that had been best embodied by the story behind burning the boats. "It did give us something to point to throughout the year," Bavis says.

"I don't know that any team lives to those standards all the time. The words meant the most when something was on the line, whether it was a Beanpot championship or a Hockey East championship. That's where those guys did live it. You look at all the pitfalls and setbacks that you have as individuals and personalities. How does all that eventually get put aside when it's on the line?"

Perhaps an answer to that question can be found if we look at what historian Hugh Thomas had to say in summarizing the behavior of Cortés. "The word which best expresses Cortés' actions is 'audacity': it contains a hint of imagination, impertinence, a capacity to perform

200

the unexpected which differentiates it from mere valor."

The Terrier coaching staff showed imagination by reinventing the team's offseason preparation to encourage the BU players to elevate their game mentally and physically. Matt Gilroy proved to be an impertinent leader, pushing his coach to rethink his personnel decisions and response to the bad stretch of play in the fall.

Scoring twice in under a minute a dozen times—most notably in the most exciting last minute of NCAA ice hockey history—certainly exemplifies that capacity to perform the unexpected.

Invoking the spirit of Hernán Cortés, let us always remember this legendary BU team for its audacity.

EPILOGUE

Within days of winning the national championship, **Matt Gilroy** finally cashed in on his status as an undrafted free agent, signing a $3.5 million contract for two years with the New York Rangers. This will give him a chance to play regularly in the arena where his father once played basketball for St. John's. "All I have is an opportunity, which I had here," Gilroy says. "If I'm willing to put in the time and the work—work hard and keep my mouth shut—I'll be fine.

"One reason I picked the Rangers was because of contract reasons, but there were a bunch of teams at the same level as them. I also love Coach [John] Tortorella. He's pretty crazy, but he's a passionate guy. The thing I love most about him is that he's honest—tells it like it is. He's kind of like Coach Parker, who you butt heads with sometimes but he makes you a better player. That's what I'm hoping Coach Tortorella can do for me, too. If I didn't come to BU, I wouldn't be the player I am now. Here, they make you a better player and a better person."

As expected, **Colin Wilson** decided to forego his last two years of collegiate eligibility to sign with the

Nashville Predators. For months, Parker had been joking about how he needed to get everything he could out of the sophomore this year as it had become obvious that he was ready for the next level. The BU coach's philosophy with players going pro is that he has no problem with it if the player has an excellent chance of going directly to the NHL. However, he sees no point in players leaving to play in the AHL.

Which brings us to **Brian Strait**. When I spoke to Strait in May, I admittedly didn't ask him about whether he might forego his senior season to turn pro. Although he had been drafted by the Pittsburgh Penguins, and I had heard talk that he and Nick Bonino were not sure if they would stay or go, I didn't believe that Strait would leave and thus didn't ask him.

I was wrong. Although he had been named co-captain of the 2009-10 Terriers along with **Kevin Shattenkirk**, Strait opted to sign with the Penguins. When I spoke to Parker about it, he told me that he hoped that Strait would play in the NHL for the majority of next season… but he appeared skeptical as to whether it was the right move. "It remains to be seen whether it's the correct decision for him," Parker said.

Asked if Strait may enjoy some financial advantage by leaving now, Parker replied, "I don't see any at all." He pointed out that Strait could have opted for free agency late in the summer of 2010 if the Penguins didn't make an offer to his liking by then, potentially making more money that way. Strait also will miss out on the experience of being a senior and captain. In any event, Parker admitted that the team would miss Strait's leadership and strong play as a defensive defenseman next season. Strait's departure leaves Shattenkirk as the first junior to be the sole captain of the Terriers since Bob Smith in the 1961-62 season.

In late June, associate head coach **David Quinn** opted to move on to the professional ranks, taking a job as the head coach of the Lake Erie Monsters, an AHL affiliate of the Colorado Avalanche. At Lake Erie, Quinn will replace former Terrier Joe Sacco, who earned a promotion to become head coach of the Avalanche.

A month later, **Mike Bavis** was promoted to associate head coach, while Buddy Powers was hired to be the new assistant coach. Among others, Quinn and Bavis should be candidates to replace Parker when he eventually steps down. Parker has emphasized that the next coach will definitely be a BU alumnus.

Among the other seniors, **John McCarthy** was the first to sign professionally. He had been drafted by the San Jose Sharks and signed with them in the spring. He probably will play much of next season in the AHL, but he has a chance to play in the NHL as a defensive specialist and penalty killer.

Back when he was 11 or 12, **Jason Lawrence** had a hockey coach named Barry Armstrong who asked his players to write down their goals for the next five or ten years. According to his mom, Anne, Jason wrote down the following:

- Prep school
- U.S. National Development Team
- Boston University
- NHL
- What a life!

Lawrence used masking tape to put the list near his bed. "We thought nothing of it," Anne Lawrence says. Eventually, though, J-Lo earned a scholarship to Cushing Academy before moving on to the U.S. Under-18 team. While he was there, he finished his career with a gold medal at the U-18 championships. Next he crossed BU off of his list of goals, once again winning the biggest prize in his final game. Then he parlayed his team lead in goal scoring into an invitation to the Boston Bruins development camp during the summer. I spoke to Mrs. Lawrence over Labor Day weekend. "As we speak today, Jason's up in Canada trying out for the Bruins. It's been quite a journey and a wonderful ride. The dream lives on."

Brandon Yip endured a bit of a waiting game after the season ended, as the Colorado Avalanche—the team that had drafted him—needed to determine who its new general manager would be before any personnel decisions were made. He finally signed with the Avalanche in July. He could very well start his professional career playing for David Quinn on Lake Erie in the AHL, but I believe he will end up in the NHL if he can stay healthy. It could even happen this season.

Also in July, **Chris Higgins** signed an AHL contract with the Syracuse Crunch, an affiliate of the Columbus Blue Jackets organization. Ironically, one of his Crunch teammates will be Miami defenseman Kevin Roeder, the player who partially blocked Colby Cohen's shot before it went into the goal in overtime of the national championship game.

Steve Smolinsky told me that his teammates were urging him to keep playing but that he was undecided as of mid-May. I envision him playing in Europe or maybe in Australia, where former teammates Eric Thomassian and Craig Sanders are one-two on their team in scoring after struggling to play regularly as BU players.

After leading the nation with a +29 plus/minus rating, **Nick Bonino** opted to return to BU for his junior year at least. Parker told him that he thought he would benefit developmentally from one more collegiate year. Bonino underwent surgery in May for a torn subsheath in his wrist, as that injury had been a nuisance all year. Look for him to get tons of ice time as the No. 1 center on the team all season.

The rest of the BU underclassmen will return. **Kieran Millan** was drafted in the fifth round of the 2009 NHL

Draft in June. Already owning the rights to **Kevin Shattenkirk** and **Colby Cohen**, the Colorado Avalanche selected the goaltender. However, he will not go pro anytime soon.

Millan starts the year as the No. 1 goalie, but I expect **Grant Rollheiser** will get ample opportunity to play during the fall. Despite Millan's phenomenal year, I believe that there could be a platoon all year, or either of those two goalies could win the right to play the majority of the games down the stretch. The BU hockey program is nothing if not a meritocracy. "I had three great goalies to work with," Geragosian says, including third-string netminder Adam Kraus in the group though Kraus did not see any game action this year. "In all of my ten years at BU, I never before took pictures with my goalies before this year. I personally like these three kids, and I hope they all stay and that I continue to work with them."

The team's defensive corps will be a strength again this coming year with **Eric Gryba** and **David Warsofsky** returning in addition to Colby Cohen and Shattenkirk. The biggest question on the team will be with the forwards, given that five of the six players on the team's top two scoring lines are now gone. In addition to Bonino, **Zach Cohen** should be ready for much more ice time than he's ever had before as a Terrier. The sophomore trio of **Chris Connolly, Vinny Saponari,** and **Corey Trivino** will be expected to step up, and they should see much more power-play time, giving them the opportunity to do so. **Joe Pereira** and **Luke Popko** likely will continue to play valuable roles. Perhaps the most interesting development will be to see who works the hardest out of **Kevin Gilroy, Andrew Glass,** and **Victor Saponari** in the battle for ice time. Sophomore **Ross Gaudet** did not see any game action during 2008-09 but could work his way into the mix as well. There is a strong recruiting class as usual, so the returning players are by no means a lock for the regular lineup.

Lastly, how long will **Jack Parker** keep going behind the bench? When he signed a contract extension several years ago, he predicted he would bow out before it was over. Now, though, he shows no indication of calling it quits anytime soon. His contract right now goes through 2013. "The thing that's amazed me is that a whole bunch of people have said 'Geez, I thought this would be the year you retire—go out on top,'" Parker says. "That was the most enjoyable year we've had in a long, long time. Why would I want to stop doing that?"

That said, don't expect to see Parker coaching as an octogenarian. "I won't be [Penn State football coach] Joe Paterno [who turned 82 in December and is still coaching]. This time of year, everyone has fun as a college hockey coach—June, July, August. I don't think it is *ever* fun during the season. It's a hard job. But one of the reasons I think coaches get along so well is that nobody knows how difficult it is except the guy across the bench. It's hard on your family; it's hard on your stomach. Some people handle it differently, but no matter how you handle it, it's hard.

"As Tim Taylor has always said, the W's never outweigh the losses. The losses linger with you and the wins disappear"—Parker snaps his fingers—"because you've got your next game."

For the coming season, David Quinn made an apt comment before moving on to Lake Erie. "Next year we don't need to be as good as last year's team. We just need to be better than everybody else."

In all probability, no team in college hockey will be as good next year as BU was this year. I suspect that no program will have the opportunity to win seven titles, let alone actually winning them all. It may be a very long time before it happens again, if it happens at all.

Regardless, everyone associated with Boston University hockey will still be reminiscing about any number of great moments over the course of a magical year:

- The young defensemen leading the charge with a one-two punch of shorthanded goals to finish off the Huskies in the Beanpot.

- Zach Cohen powering his way from the corner to the net to score the first of three goals in 44 seconds against BC in the Hockey East semifinals.

- Kieran Millan looking absolutely unflappable in the Hockey East championship game and the NCAA Regional against UNH, winning both games when his teammates struggled to score.

- Jason Lawrence's "hand of God" goal in the same UNH game.

- Colin Wilson and Chris Higgins stepping up against Vermont in the semifinal, while the defense clamped down to carry Kieran Millan as much as he had carried them for so much of the season.

- The two goals in under one minute—yet again against Miami, punctuated by Matt Gilroy's presence under pressure to make the pass of a lifetime.

- The BU bench exploding as one in response to Nick Bonino scoring the biggest goal in BU hockey history.

- Finally, the slick pass of Kevin Shattenkirk to tee it up for Colby Cohen's partially blocked slapper, knuckling its way into the net.

Whatever their favorite moment may be, players, coaches, staff, and fans will never tire of recounting it all. For decades to come, the small, warm world of college hockey will laud the team that burned the boats and conquered everyone in their path, winning it all with a heart of Mexican gold.

APPENDIX

Boston University 2008-09 Schedule and Results

Sunday	10/5/2008	NEW BRUNSWICK (exhibition)	W	4-1
Friday	10/10/2008	NORTH DAKOTA (Ice Breaker)	W	5-1
Saturday	10/11/2008	MICHIGAN STATE (Ice Breaker)	W	2-1
Friday	10/17/2008	MERRIMACK	W	5-2
Sunday	10/19/2008	@New Hampshire	L	1-2
Saturday	10/25/2008	MICHIGAN	W	7-2
Saturday	11/1/2008	@Vermont	W	7-2
Friday	11/7/2008	@UMass Lowell	W	6-4
Friday	11/14/2008	MASSACHUSETTS	L	6-5
Sunday	11/16/2008	NORTHEASTERN	W	3-0
Friday	11/21/2008	VERMONT	L	3-4
Saturday	11/22/2008	VERMONT	L	3-4
Tuesday	11/25/2008	HOLY CROSS	W	3-2
Saturday	11/29/2008	ST. LAWRENCE	W	4-1
Friday	12/5/2008	BOSTON COLLEGE	T	1-1 (ot)
Saturday	12/6/2008	@Boston College	W	3-1
Friday	12/12/2008	UMASS LOWELL	W	3-2
Friday	1/2/2009	vs. Rensselaer (Denver Cup)	W	6-2
Saturday	1/3/2009	@Denver (Denver Cup)	W	4-1
Saturday	1/10/2009	MAINE	W	4-1
Tuesday	1/13/2009	PROVIDENCE	L	2-4
Friday	1/16/2009	@Merrimack	W	4-1
Saturday	1/17/2009	BOSTON COLLEGE	W	5-2
Friday	1/23/2009	NEW HAMPSHIRE	W	5-0
Saturday	1/24/2009	@New Hampshire	W	3-1
Friday	1/30/2009	@Merrimack	W	3-1
Monday	2/2/2009	vs. Harvard (Beanpot)	W	4-3
Friday	2/6/2009	UMASS LOWELL	W	5-3
Monday	2/9/2009	vs. Northeastern (Beanpot Final)	W	5-2
Friday	2/13/2009	@Maine	W	7-2

Saturday	2/14/2009	@Maine	T	2-2 (ot)
Friday	2/20/2009	NORTHEASTERN	T	2-2 (ot)
Saturday	2/21/2009	@Northeastern	T	1-1 (ot)
Friday	2/27/2009	@Massachusetts	W	7-3
Saturday	2/28/2009	MASSACHUSETTS	W	7-2
Friday	3/6/2009	@Providence	W	8-2
Sunday	3/8/2009	PROVIDENCE	W	3-0
Friday	3/13/2009	MAINE (HE Quarterfinals)	W	2-1
Saturday	3/14/2009	MAINE (HE Quarterfinals)	L	3-6
Sunday	3/15/2009	MAINE (HE Quarterfinals)	W	6-2
Friday	3/20/2009	vs. Boston College (HE Semifinals)	W	3-2
Saturday	3/21/2009	vs. UMass Lowell (HE Final)	W	1-0
Saturday	3/28/2009	vs. Ohio State (Northeast Regional)	W	8-3
Sunday	3/29/2009	vs. New Hampshire (Northeast Regional)	W	2-1
Thursday	4/9/2009	vs. Vermont (National Semifinal)	W	5-4
Saturday	4/11/2009	vs. Miami (National Championship)	W	4-3 (ot)

Boston University Records	
Overall:	35-6-4 (177 GF, 91 GA)
Hockey East:	18-5-4 (103 GF, 54 GA)
Home:	16-4-2 (83 GF, 43 GA)
Away:	10-2-2 (56 GF, 28 GA)
Overtime:	1-0-4

2008-09 Roster

No.	Name	Class	Pos.	Ht.	Wt.	Hometown
2	Eric Gryba	JR	D	6'4"	215	Saskatoon, Sask.
3	Kevin Shattenkirk	SO	D	5'11"	200	New Rochelle, N.Y.
4	Ryan Ruikka	FR	D	6'1"	187	Chelsea, Mich.
5	David Warsofsky	FR	D	5'9"	170	Marshfield, Mass.
6	Joe Pereira	SO	F	5'10"	185	West Haven, Conn.
7	Brian Strait	JR	D	6'1"	205	Waltham, Mass.
8	Steve Smolinsky	SR	F	5'10"	175	Plymouth, Mass.
9	Corey Trivino	FR	F	6'1"	175	Toronto, Ont.
10	Chris Higgins	SR	F	5'11"	185	Lynnfield, Mass.
11	Zach Cohen	JR	F	6'3"	215	Schaumburg, Ill.
12	Chris Connolly	FR	F	5'9"	165	Duluth, Minn.
13	Nick Bonino	SO	F	6'1"	190	Unionville, Conn.
14	Andrew Glass	FR	F	5'11"	180	Wrentham, Mass.
15	John McCarthy	SR	F	6'1"	198	Andover, Mass.
16	Kevin Gilroy	FR	F	6'0"	185	North Bellmore, N.Y.
17	Victor Saponari	SO	F	5'10"	176	Powder Springs, Ga.
18	Brandon Yip	SR	F	6'1"	197	Maple Ridge, B.C.
21	Jason Lawrence	SR	F	5'10"	185	Saugus, Mass.
22	Ross Gaudet	FR	F	6'0"	185	Burlington, Mass.
25	Colby Cohen	SO	D	6'3"	210	Villanova, Pa.
26	Luke Popko	JR	F	5'10"	204	Skillman, N.J.
27	Vinny Saponari	FR	F	6'0"	180	Powder Springs, Ga.
31	Kieran Millan	FR	G	6'0"	190	Edmonton, Alta.
32	Adam Kraus	SO	G	6'3"	187	Irving, Texas
33	Colin Wilson	SO	F	6'2"	215	Winnipeg, Man.
35	Grant Rollheiser	FR	G	6'4"	195	Chilliwack, B.C.
97	Matt Gilroy	SR	D	6'2"	202	North Bellmore, N.Y.

Individual Statistics

Scoring	Overall - 45 GP (35-6-4 .822)									
Player	GP	G	A	PTS	+/-	PIM	SOG	PPG	SHG	GWG
Colin Wilson	43	17	38	55	21	52	105	6	1	5
Nick Bonino	44	18	32	50	29	30	114	7	1	1
Chris Higgins	42	14	34	48	17	40	77	3	2	2
Brandon Yip	45	20	23	43	24	118	131	4	1	3
Jason Lawrence	44	25	14	39	18	38	115	14	0	8
Matt Gilroy	45	8	29	37	22	12	91	5	1	2
Colby Cohen	43	8	24	32	24	65	59	6	0	3
Chris Connolly	45	10	20	30	9	12	94	2	1	3
John McCarthy	45	6	23	29	16	24	80	0	1	0
Kevin Shattenkirk	43	7	21	28	28	40	93	3	1	1
David Warsofsky	45	3	20	23	26	28	95	1	1	0
Zach Cohen	41	13	5	18	10	22	82	0	0	2
Vinny Saponari	44	8	9	17	6	39	58	2	0	2
Luke Popko	45	5	9	14	10	24	41	0	0	1
Corey Trivino	32	6	7	13	10	14	19	1	0	1
Joe Pereira	34	3	7	10	5	74	20	0	0	1
Brian Strait	38	2	5	7	10	67	32	1	0	0
Eric Gryba	45	0	6	6	21	106	26	0	0	0
Andrew Glass	15	2	1	3	3	2	12	0	0	0
Kevin Gilroy	12	2	0	2	-3	2	17	0	0	0
Steve Smolinsky	14	0	1	1	2	0	8	0	0	0
Victor Saponari	5	0	0	0	1	2	1	0	0	0
Grant Rollheiser	12	0	0	0	4	0	0	0	0	0
Kieran Millan	35	0	0	0	58	0	0	0	0	0
Boston University Totals	45	177	328	505	65	823	1370	55	10	35
Opponent Totals	45	91	146	237	-65	792	1068	34	4	6

Goaltending	GP	GA	Saves	Shots	Save%	GAA	Record	Win%	GS	SO
Kieran Millan	35	67	776	843	.921	1.94	29-2-3	.897	35	3
Grant Rollheiser	12	23	201	224	.897	2.13	6-4-1	.591	10	1
Boston University Totals	45	91	977	1068	.915	2	35-6-4	.822	45	4
Opponent Totals	45	177	1193	1370	.871	3.89	6-35-4	.178	45	0

TEAM STATISTICS

2008-09 Boston University Men's Hockey
Overall Team Statistics - All Games

Overall: 35-6-4 Conf: 18-5-4 Home: 16-4-2 Away: 10-2-2 Neutral: 9-0-0

TEAM STATISTICS	BU	OPP
SHOT STATISTICS		
Goals-Shot attempts	177-1370	91-1068
Shot pct	0.129	0.085
Goals/Game	3.9	2
Shots/Game	30.4	23.7
POWER PLAYS		
Goals-Power Plays	55-251	34-270
Conversion Percent	0.219	0.126
GOAL BREAKDOWN		
Total Goals	177	91
Power Play	55	34
Short-handed	10	4
Empty net	5	1
Penalty shot	1	0
Unassisted	2	8
Overtime	1	0
PENALTIES		
Number	357	335
Minutes	823	792
FACEOFFS (W-L)	1400-1372	1372-1400
Faceoff W-L Pct	0.505	0.495

GOALS BY PERIOD	1	2	3	OT	Total
Boston University	59	55	62	1	177
Opponents	25	37	29	0	91

SHOTS BY PERIOD	1	2	3	OT	Total
Boston University	466	485	396	23	1,370
Opponents	359	340	350	19	1,068

SAVES BY PERIOD	1	2	3	OT	Total
Boston University	334	303	321	19	977
Opponents	407	430	334	22	1,193

212